# Beyond the Answer Sheet:

# Beyond the Answer Sheet:

◆

## Academic Success for International Students

*William B. Badke*

iUniverse, Inc.
New York  Lincoln  Shanghai

# Beyond the Answer Sheet:
## Academic Success for International Students

iUniverse, Inc.

For information address:
iUniverse, Inc.
2021 Pine Lake Road, Suite 100
Lincoln, NE 68512
www.iuniverse.com

ISBN: 0-595-27196-0

Printed in the United States of America

# *Contents*

INTRODUCTION What you will learn from this book . . . . . . . . . 1

CHAPTER 1    A Different Way of Thinking about
Education . . . . . . . . . . . . . . . . . . . . . . . . . . . . . . . 5

CHAPTER 2    The skills you need to succeed . . . . . . . . . . . . . . . 16

CHAPTER 3    The Classroom—New Ways of Learning . . . . . . 30

CHAPTER 4    The Classroom—Syllabus, Notes and
Assignments . . . . . . . . . . . . . . . . . . . . . . . . . . . . 45

CHAPTER 5    Professors . . . . . . . . . . . . . . . . . . . . . . . . . . . . . . 58

CHAPTER 6    The Library . . . . . . . . . . . . . . . . . . . . . . . . . . . . 71

CHAPTER 7    Writing Research Papers . . . . . . . . . . . . . . . . . . 87

EXCURSUS—What's the Big Problem with Plagiarism? . . . . . . . . 97

CHAPTER 8    Other Types of Assignments—Reading
Assignments, Book Reviews, Journals,
Reflection Papers, Group Projects, Seminar
Presentations, Class Participation . . . . . . . . . . . 105

CHAPTER 9    Quizzes and Examinations. . . . . . . . . . . . . . . . . 118

CHAPTER 10   Important People to Know in your Academic
World . . . . . . . . . . . . . . . . . . . . . . . . . . . . . . . . . . 126

CONCLUSION Encouragement. . . . . . . . . . . . . . . . . . . . . . . . . 137

APPENDIX    Graduate Study and Thesis Work. . . . . . . . . . . . 141

Index. . . . . . . . . . . . . . . . . . . . . . . . . . . . . . . . . . . . . . . . . . . . . . 151

# INTRODUCTION
## *What you will learn from this book*

You have just travelled many hours to a new country. Right now you feel as if you have landed on the moon, because everything is so strange.

There are sounds of loudspeakers saying words to you that you do not understand. Hundreds, even thousands, of people not of your culture or race are walking through the airport area. All of them seem to know where they are going and what they need to do. Most of them are speaking the same language as the loudspeakers are, but speaking it more clearly. You suddenly recognize that soon you will have to speak this language too. English conversation will no longer be an exercise in a language classroom but an important part of real life.

You hope the people who promised to meet you will be there and that they can find you. You hope that at least one of them speaks your own language and that no one will ask you too many questions, because you are tired and you know your English is not as good you would like it to be.

You hope you have not made a terrible mistake coming to this strange land to study at this school so far from home. For the moment you are lonely and nervous.

> The purpose of this book is to help you succeed as an international student in a Western school of higher education. It will explain to you what you need to know and what skills you need to develop to survive your experience in the classroom and the library. It will also guide you into methods you can use to get good results with your assignments and examinations.

Before we go any farther, however, let me explain what this book will *not* do. It will *not* tell you:

- What school to attend
- How to deal with immigration officials, visas, and so on
- How to find housing
- How to earn money while you are a student
- How to register for courses

There are other books that can teach you about such things.

This book, however, will help you understand what is required of you as a *student* and how to do well in your studies. I cannot guarantee that you will receive high grades, because high grades also require your own hard work. What I can guarantee is that, if you follow the advice of this book, you will be much better prepared to succeed as a student, knowing what is demanded of you and understanding how to meet those demands.

In the following pages, I will teach you:

- What Western education is all about—its philosophy and what it demands of you.
- What you will experience in the classroom, and how to make that experience successful.
- What Western libraries are like and how they work

- How to complete assignments, essays and examinations according to Western requirements.

- How to have a good experience dealing with your professors.

- What critical thinking requires.

- How to feel comfortable as a student in the West.

Many students have already done what you are doing—studied in the West. But most of them discovered the methods and rules of Western education simply by experience.

This book will give you the opportunity to learn about our ways of education before you enter the classroom or the library, and before you need to write an essay or an examination. Such knowledge can greatly improve your hope for success.

# 1

## *A Different Way of Thinking about Education*

What is a Western education? What are its main features? How is it different from the education you may have experienced in your home country?

To answer, we need first to look at the difference between the approach to education in the West and the approach to education in most of the rest of the world. Then we need to understand what is important to teachers in the West, and finally what methods are used to make Western education succeed.

The following information may seem to explain everything about the educational differences in the West. You need to understand, however, that while I am saying some rather general things about the main differences between most non-Western and Western education, none of what I am describing is found in every situation. It is intended only as a basic guide to two different ways of thinking about teaching and learning. There is no guarantee that such patterns will be found in every classroom. As other parts of the world continue to take on Western concepts of education, the differences found in the West may one day be much less important than they are now. But right now, they are significant.

## Western Education is Different

I spent two years teaching at a college in West Africa. Every day as I drove to work I passed elementary schools and high schools in which most of the students were doing the same activity. The teacher would shout something and the students would shout it back. The teacher would repeat it and then the students would shout it again.

They were memorizing. The method of repeating information aloud was a good one, because it involved the whole body and thus made memorization easier. In your country, you may not have shouted aloud in answer to your teacher when you were learning, but memorization was likely a major part of your daily activity. If you went to university, memorization continued. In fact, your professors may have measured your intelligence by your ability to remember facts. If you had a good memory, you were intelligent; if you forgot easily, you were not.

In many countries of the world, memorization is the main skill needed to gain a good education. Memory is important in such an educational system, because the system is based on the fact that your culture has existed for thousands of years, with knowledge being passed down from generation to generation as a treasured heritage. In each generation the knowledge grows a little bit as some new information is added, but the main task of the student is to learn the traditions, thus to memorize. When the next generation learns and understands the knowledge of its society, there is a guarantee that the traditions will not be lost. In societies like this, simply knowing facts is valued very highly, and neglecting to pass on facts can be a disaster. Let me give you an example:

When I was in Africa, people would point to this plant or that, and say, "You could eat that." This seemed very strange to me, because people said it to me so often, and it was always a different type of plant that they were pointing to. Why would they find it so important to tell me what plants I could eat? They knew I had lots of food and would likely never actually need to pick one of those plants from the side of the road and eat it.

The answer was that there had been a civil war ten years before, and the people were forced to leave their homes in the cities to hide in the jungle. In earlier centuries, their ancestors had known what was safe to eat in the jungle, but the knowledge had been lost because city dwellers did not think it was something they needed to pass on to their children. The people who fled from their cities into the jungle knew they would soon starve if they did not discover what they could eat and what was poisonous. So they began cooking various plants and feeding them to their chickens. If the chickens lived, that was a plant you could eat. If the chickens died, the plant was poisonous. In this way, the people gradually recovered the knowledge they had lost. Now, ten years later, they wanted to share their knowledge with me, even though they had since returned to their cities. When they said, "You could eat that," they were telling me how much they treasured their knowledge, and they were showing me that they intended never to forget it again.

## The Discipleship Model

In most of the world, knowledge is strength. If I can learn what is passed down to me by my parents and teachers, then I will have the understanding that will help me survive and be successful in my society. This is why, in much of the world, education is simply the passing on of knowledge. The teacher communicates what needs to be known, and the student learns it, often by memorization.

This is what we might call a "Discipleship Model" of education.

> THE DISCIPLESHIP MODEL: The teacher, who is an expert or master in a certain kind of knowledge, passes on that knowledge to students who are expected, during their lifetimes, to become great in knowledge themselves so that they can teach the next generation in turn.

Thus the centuries pass, each generation taking the responsibility to make sure the next generation receives and learns well the knowledge of the society. The Discipleship Model, which goes back many thousands of years, has always been a proven method of preserving the truths that a society lives by.

Under the Discipleship Model, teachers are highly honored as the guardians and instructors of the valued knowledge of the society. Why would such people not be given the highest respect? Truly, a society that treats its teachers badly will soon know nothing.

Teachers within the Discipleship Model tend to be very serious people. They demand much of their students and are often stern in their criticisms. But students continue to respect and honor their teachers, understanding that education is indeed a serious thing that will determine the future of their society. To mock or criticize the teacher who possesses the knowledge would be seen as an act of rebellion, an evil deed that is unforgivable.

In the Discipleship Model, the writers of books and articles are honored as well. The student does not criticize what a great writer has written, even if it may seem to be in error. Such criticisms, if they are made, should come from teachers, not students. The teacher or professor will tell you what you should believe about a certain writing and what is incorrect.

In fact, in many cultures outside of the West, controversy and disagreements in the classroom are not encouraged. If I suggested to my African students that there were several points of view on a certain issue, the students' hands would immediately go up, and they would ask, "But sir, what's the *right* view?" They expected me to tell them how to end the controversy by giving them the answer so that they could add to their knowledge.

In the Discipleship Model, the rule is that the professor deals with the controversies, finds the solutions and passes those solutions on to students. This rule continues to be in effect until a student begins working on a masters or doctoral thesis. At that point, the thesis advisor begins to train the student in thinking critically, evaluating, and making judgments. As the student writes the thesis, he or she is being prepared to become an expert in the field who is qualified to teach others.

Knowledge is the whole purpose of the Discipleship Model of education. Debate and disagreement by undergraduate and even beginning graduate students does not add to knowledge, because these students are not yet *qualified* to evaluate and judge in areas of controversy. That is the task of the teacher, not the student. The student is there to learn, not to solve problems.

## The Western Model

In North America, Australia, and parts of Europe, the Discipleship Model of education is almost unknown. This is something that you need to understand well—*the Western Model of education is very different from the Discipleship Model of the rest of the world.* In the Western Model, the goal of education is not to gain knowledge but to use knowledge to solve problems.

> THE WESTERN MODEL: In the West, we do not really value knowledge unless we are convinced that it will be useful.

This is very important to understand. Knowledge in the West is not valued just because it is knowledge. Only certain parts of our knowledge are valued—the parts that we believe to be useful to us. Why is this the case?

- Some people have suggested that this philosophy of knowledge exists because Western cultures are not very old. Most people in North America and Australia came to those lands within the past hundred and fifty years. They created a new culture different from the many cultures in which they originated. Thus they have no long tradition of knowledge.

- Some have suggested that Westerners tend to be independent thinkers. They left their traditional cultures behind because they wanted to live a new life in their own way. This means that they tend to challenge traditional knowledge and only value it when they find it useful.

- The most likely reason why the West does not value knowledge unless it is viewed as useful, is that knowledge in the West has increased and changed to a much greater degree than in other cultures where tradition is more valued. Westerners have come to understand that it is impossible to learn even a small part of their knowledge base, because knowledge grows so quickly. Thus they must choose only the knowledge that is useful to them. If this is, indeed, the reason why the Western Model exists, the rest of the world will probably one day also move to this approach and away from the Discipleship Model as non-Western cultures experience the same rapid growth in knowledge. But right now, the Discipleship Model is still strong, except in the West.

In addition to the fact that the Western Model of education tends only to value useful knowledge, this model also encourages critical thinking even at the beginning undergraduate level—the kind of thinking that evaluates information to discover whether it is good or bad, valid or invalid, useful or useless. The Discipleship Model values critical thinking as well, but it is *the teacher*, not the student, who is supposed to do this task. In the Western Model, *both teacher and students* are encouraged to use critical thinking.

This can create great confusion for students who are familiar only with the Discipleship Model. They have been told in their home countries that they are not qualified to criticize and evaluate. Now, in a Western setting, they are told that criticism and evaluation are required.

I was recently explaining to a student from Asia that a research paper assignment asked her to begin with a research question and use evidence to discover the answer to the question. She responded, "But surely the professor will give me an answer sheet." I asked her what she meant. She said, "An answer sheet for the research paper, so I will know what the answer is supposed to be." I had to explain to her that there would be no answer sheet. If she asked her professor what the answer to her research question was supposed to be, the professor would not give her one. She was expected to find the answer herself, even though there were several possible answers and the topic was very controversial.

The highest value in Western education is critical thinking. This does not mean negative thinking in which we react against every idea or piece of knowledge we are given. Rather, it means *evaluating everything that we are taught in order to determine whether it is valid or not. It means investigating areas of controversy in order to determine what is most likely the information that we should trust or believe. It means considering evidence that is presented in support of a point of view in order to determine whether the evidence is good or not, or to determine if another point of view is better supported by the evidence.*

In the Discipleship Model of education, critical thinking is the responsibility of the teacher. In the Western Model, it is the responsibility of the student. The teacher may provide guidance, but each student is expected to do his or her own evaluation.

During the past few decades, however, the philosophy of **Postmodernism** has begun to change the Western Model. While earlier generations of professors emphasized rational and critical thinking, Postmodernism has taught us to distrust the power of the mind to discover truth. Postmodernism argues that each of us has our own experience of reality so that the concept of truth as something all of us can accept equally does not exist. We all have our own version of "truth," based on who we are and what our experiences have been.

The result for Western education has been less of an emphasis on the mind and more of an stress on personal experience. For example, we were once taught in a poetry class to determine the message that the author was trying to communicate through the poem, because this was the "truth" contained in that poem. Now, a student may be taught to do what is called "Reader Response Criticism," where each reader's personal reaction to a poem and understanding of it are more important than what the author intended to communicate.

Critical thinking still remains a high value, but you may at times be asked not to evaluate information with the techniques of reason but instead to reveal your personal reaction or your feelings about the things you are studying. Or you may be told that truth can never be known for certain and that the best we can hope for is that the evidence supports one view better than another.

This, again, can be disturbing to a student who is used to the Discipleship Model. You are used to being taught that the knowledge given to you by your professor is true and certain. It is not to be challenged or doubted, because the professor, as the expert, has done all the evaluation that is needed and has declared to you that it is true. The Western Model, while encouraging students to discover what is reliable and certain, has now been influenced by doubts that truth can ever be found.

If you have been taught by the Discipleship Model, you will likely now be thinking that the original Western Model and Postmodernism contradict one another. They do. The Western Model was created to trust the mind to discover truth through a process of critical thinking. Postmodernism says one single truth cannot be found.

The way in which these two views work together is by accepting both at the same time. We in the West still value the work of critical thinking—judging evidence, evaluating information, discovering which point of view is most likely—but we also take into account the reality that each of us experiences knowledge in a different way. This means that when we reach a conclusion through critical thinking, not everyone will accept that conclusion. Others may disagree with us and view the evidence in a different way, thus coming to a different conclusion.

For Western education, the mixing of the Western Model with Postmodernism means that discussion and debate are almost endless. You as a student may write a research paper or present a viewpoint in class, only to have the professor disagree. But the professor's view is not absolute either. Thus you have the right to present your view again and (politely) challenge the professor's belief about the topic.

The fact that your professor or fellow students do not agree with you is not a disaster. As long as you show good skill in presenting the evidence for the view you hold, you can still do well in the classroom even if the professor does not accept your view. There are exceptions, of course, where some professors will make it difficult for students who do not share their beliefs, but this is rare. In most situations, the professor is more interested in how you present your case than in what you conclude.

At the same time, each discipline (major subject of study) does have its own boundaries, methods and language. There are still rules about how you discuss topics, present information, and write essays. What you will see in the classroom is not chaos but the exchange of ideas within definite limitations. You will learn about these as you observe your professor and fellow students.

## The Two Models Contrasted

In summary form, let us consider the differences between the Discipleship Model and the Western Model of education:

DISCIPLESHIP MODEL                              WESTERN MODEL

| Discipleship Model | Western Model |
|---|---|
| Knowledge is highly valued | Knowledge is valued only if useful |
| Professor does the critical thinking | Professor & student do the critical thinking |
| Student is expected to learn, not criticize | Student is expected to analyze everything |
| Memorization is very important | Memorization is less important |
| Intelligence measured by memory ability | Intelligence measured by analytical ability |
| Certainty and truth are possible | All "truth" is open to challenge |

## *Imagine*

STUDENT: Professor, Johnson?

PROF: Yes?

STUDENT: You said I should come to your office if I have a problem.

PROF: Yes, what is your difficulty?

STUDENT: It is this research essay. You said I needed to develop a research question, consider the evidence, and use it to answer the question. But I don't see any list of research questions.

PROF: There isn't any list. I want you to find your own question.

STUDENT: My own?

PROF: Do some reading, find some controversy, then answer that controversy. Let me give you an example: Your essay is supposed to examine one or more philosophies used in environmentalism. You could create a research question like this: *How valid is Lynn White's critique of the Judeo-Christian heritage as a cause for the environmental crisis?*

STUDENT: Lynn White. We studied his article in class the other day. You said that several criticisms of it had been made. I think I have notes.

PROF: Well, that's the sort of thing you could ask as a research question—How valid is Lynn White's critique?

STUDENT: Could I use that one?

PROF: I'd rather you choose one of your own, but if you really want to use it, I can't stop you.

STUDENT: Are you saying yes or no?

PROF: Yes.

STUDENT: In class, you didn't give the answer.

PROF: The answer to what?

STUDENT: To the question about Lynn White.

PROF: No, I didn't. That's why this would be a good topic for your paper. You need to find the answer yourself.

STUDENT: But I know very little about it. What if I find the wrong answer?

PROF: Wrong in what way?

STUDENT: If I decide Lynn White's argument is correct, but you believe he is wrong.

PROF: (Giving an encouraging look) This is very confusing, isn't it? You probably feel like I'm playing some sort of game by not giving you the answer. I'm not. I want you to learn how to think about the philosophy of environmentalism. I want you to learn how to evaluate, make judgments. If I tell you the answer, then you don't need to think.

STUDENT: But I'm still untrained.

PROF: And this is how you will become trained—by looking at evidence and evaluating it so that you can answer questions for yourself.

STUDENT: It seems very difficult.

PROF: Let's look at the assignment again and I'll help you get started. After that, it's up to you. But don't worry. I know you can do it.

# 2

## *The skills you need to succeed*

You have faced many challenges since you left your familiar homeland for a strange land where there are surprises everywhere. The classroom is the one place that you believe should feel like home in a Western school. After all, you've attended classes almost all your life.

But when you get into a Western classroom, you find that many things are new. The professor does not lecture all the time—there are discussion groups, student presentations, and a great deal of interaction between professor and students. The professor may tell jokes and seem very casual. The students may appear to be disrespectful and far less serious about their education than they should be. You may not understand everything that is said. The assignments you are given may not make sense to you.

The library will seem enormous, full of books, but also of journals, microfiche, and, most disturbing of all, computers linked to databases that you have never encountered before. There is an information desk, but you do not feel brave enough to ask any questions from the person sitting there. Everyone else seems to know what to do in this strange library, but you don't. Even the way the books are organized on the shelves is unfamiliar.

Everywhere in this school you will hear the same message—*finding answers is your responsibility. No one will do your thinking for you.* You long for the days when education meant listening to the professor, memorizing the material and writing essays in which the solution was plain before you began. You wish you could have examinations that test your memory, not your ability to analyze.

None of what I have just described is intended to frighten you. Western education is not impossible. It simply demands that you develop another set of skills that will help you succeed. It is the purpose of this chapter to explain those skills and to show you how to make them a strong part of your life.

So let's begin. What are the skills you need to develop to survive your Western education and find success?

## Courage

I have always admired international students. You have left a place you once called "home" and a language that was your own. Now you are a stranger in a land whose culture and language are so different that you are constantly finding yourself at a disadvantage. This is something I understand from the two years I spent in Africa. Every day and every situation there was an opportunity for me to misunderstand, say the wrong thing, do the wrong thing, and amuse those around me.

All of us have a personal sense of self-respect. None of us like to be embarrassed or made to feel incompetent or ridiculous. But living in another culture means that the next embarrassment is just around the corner. People notice us and can easily see that we are different. Some of them may be afraid of us or may not know what to say to us. Some may even have racial prejudices that hurt our feelings.

The fact that you are studying in the West demonstrates that you have courage, because it takes courage to overcome the fear of being a stranger in a new society. You have made a promise to yourself that you will endure the difficulties because the education you are seeking is more important than whether or not you feel comfortable.

But to truly succeed as a student in the West, you will need even more courage:

- Courage to refuse to spend your time only with students of your culture or language. If you and your fellow students form a social group in which you only speak your national language and find all your friendships with people of your culture, you will never understand Western education properly. You are going to need to interact with Westerners.

- Courage to try new things. Perhaps it will mean accepting an invitation to a social event where you will be the only person from your country, or starting up a conversation with a stranger whose native language is English, or answering a question in class, or agreeing to register for a course that requires you to do a twenty minute oral presentation. Every new experience is a worry, but each will strength your abilities as a student.

- Courage to risk embarrassment. You will need to have what is known as a "thick skin," that is an approach to life that doesn't worry if you become the center of attention, or are criticized, or experience the negative looks and actions of others who may not understand who you are or why you are here. Just think—if your fellow Western students were studying in your country, they would be in situations that made them appear just as foolish as you might be feeling now. Embarrassment does not last long, then it is only a memory.

- Courage to use every experience as an opportunity to learn. Never be afraid to say, "I don't know," or to ask for more information if something is unclear to you. Your courage helps you to learn the things that you need to know in order to succeed.

## Spoken English

If English is not the language of your birth, you have likely spent many hours studying it before you arrived in the West. English is a difficult language, full of many strange features and few clear rules. Just being able to read something as simple as a newspaper article in English has taken more memorizing of vocabulary and grammar than you ever could have managed.

But the real challenge has only begun. Certainly you have learned enough English to obtain a TOEFL score that meets the requirements of the institution in which you are studying, but most of your training has been in *written* rather than spoken English. This might be enough for a classroom in which the professor lectures most of the time in standard language and provides you with supplementary reading, perhaps even class notes. But you need more than good written English to be comfortable in a Western classroom in which discussion is an important element.

*Imagine* a situation like this:

PROFESSOR: And what's your take on White's approach?
YOU: Take?
PROFESSOR: Your point of view.
YOU: I am sorry. I do not understand.
PROFESSOR: Well surely you have an opinion on White.
YOU: Opinion. Yes. I do not like all of his approach.
PROFESSOR: Why not?
YOU: It's not right.
PROFESSOR: Do you have a reason for believing that?
YOU: You said there were problems with White…I'm sorry, it is difficult to explain.

At this point, you feel very helpless. In your home country, many people praised you for being intelligent. If you didn't have to answer in English in this situation, you would do very well answering your professor. But this strange language is always a barrier to showing everyone how intelligent you are.

Language will continue to be a barrier until you develop strong skills in *spoken* English. Why? Because the English that you learned for reading and for understanding a professor using standard grammar is not the English of conversation and discussion. The English of conversation is full of colloquial and slang expressions. It breaks grammar rules. And it changes regularly. Consider the following:

You are leaving class when someone says to you, "So long." *Long? What is long?* Well, actually, nothing is long. Your fellow student is just using an expression for "Goodbye." Why does he say, "So long"? I don't know. It's just something people say.

Someone in a discussion tells you, "I don't think White knew diddly about the Old Testament." Diddly? A slang expression for "anything."

To function well in the classroom, you are going to have to learn the spoken English of everyday speech, not just the formal English of writing and of lectures. This means you will have to learn colloquial and slang expressions, as well as all the casual things English speakers say to one another that are not taught in grammar books.

How can you learn everyday spoken English?

- Move out of your "comfort zone." What is a comfort zone? A comfort zone is any situation in which you feel comfortable, at ease, not anxious. For example, if you are Chinese and you are eating in a Chinese restaurant in a Chinese district of your city, it is likely that you are in a comfort zone. If you are Chinese and you are eating Greek food in a Greek part of the city, you are likely more anxious. You are outside of your comfort zone.

  It is the same with the English language. I notice that many international students spend much of their time outside of class with people of their own language and culture. This is understandable, because you are able to encourage and support one another. But it is likely that you also speak to these students in your national language rather than English. It is a comfort zone, but you will never learn everyday English if you spend most of your time not speaking it nor listening to it.

- Seek opportunities to speak conversational English with Westerners. I was in a Chinese restaurant with my son when a Chinese lady at the next table asked if she could talk to me. She explained that she had recently come from Hong Kong, and she needed to practice her English. We had a very interesting conversation, and I learned some things about Hong Kong that I had never known before. She also complimented me on my skill with chopsticks.

I was in a line-up at a college cafeteria where I was teaching, when someone behind me said, "Hello. My name is James." He was a Korean student who had just arrived in my country, and he knew that his understanding and speaking of English was not as strong as it needed to be. We had a great conversation that developed into a friendship that we share to this day, though he has now finished graduate school. Over the years, I have watched his use of spoken English improve greatly.

Such examples show people who moved out of their comfort zones. If you try to start a conversation with a Westerner, how do you know that person will not reject you? The answer is that you don't. That is why learning spoken English is such a challenge and demands courage. But be brave. Perhaps you should even explain to those you want to talk to that you need to practice English. That will make them more willing to talk. Tell others about your homeland, your life story, why you came to the West to study. They will likely be interested.

- Find a conversation partner. Many Western colleges and universities have programs where Western students volunteer to meet with international students for conversation. Go to your Student Services department and find out if such a program exists for your school. If it does, sign up and get a partner.

- Make use of Internet-based ESL listening and speaking sites. Here are some examples:

   **http://www.eslcafe.com/search/Listening/**
   **http://www.esl-lab.com/**
   **http://iteslj.org/links/ESL/Listening/**
   **http://iteslj.org/links/ESL/Speaking/**
   **http://www.eslhome.com/esl/listen/**

*NOTE: The above addresses may change. If you want to find other sites like these, go to the search engine google.com and type in either* **ESL listening** *or* **ESL speaking.**

- Use every opportunity to practice your spoken English. Evaluate what you have heard and said. Did someone use an expression that was new to you? Write it down so you can ask somebody what it means or look it up later.

# Critical Thinking

You perhaps have a friend who finds fault in everything and is constantly criticizing everyone. That is not what we mean by critical thinking.

Critical thinking is a process of evaluation that uses logic and evidence to determine whether information is correct or incorrect according to commonly accepted standards

We use forms of critical thinking all the time.

*Imagine* that you are a parent who hears a knock on the door and discovers two police officers who ask to see your eighteen year old son.

"My son is at university right now," you say. "What's the problem, officers?"

"We have reason to believe he robbed a grocery store last evening," one of them answers. "There was a video camera running in the store, and someone has identified the person on the video as your son."

You are shocked. Your son is a robber? It couldn't be. So you say to the officers, "You must have made a mistake. It wasn't my son. It couldn't have been."

The officers smile and say, "In that case we're sorry we bothered you. It must have been somebody else." *No they don't.* They say, "We have the video tape. Tell us how to find your son. He will soon be under arrest."

At this point you have no evidence to support you except the feeling in your heart that your son would not do such a thing. A feeling like that is called an "opinion." But an opinion has no real strength when it comes to finding out for sure whether information is correct. You need critical thinking.

So you ask, "What time was the store robbed last night?"

The officer looks in his notebook and says, "The video tape read 7:49 when your son was first seen on it."

"Just a few minutes before eight?" you say. "My son was at his college study group meeting in the library from 7 to 9. I can get you the phone number of the teaching assistant that was leading the group. He'll tell you my son was there all evening. So can the 9 or 10 other students who were there."

Now *that* is critical thinking—putting forward evidence in order to convince the officers that it could not have been your son because your son was somewhere else at the time. It's not based on feelings. It's not opinion. True, the officers will have to contact the leader and others who were at the meeting with your son, but the evidence will soon show that the police were incorrect in accusing him. He couldn't have robbed the store because he was at his college group meeting at the time of the robbery.

Why is critical thinking so important in Western education?

Part of the reason is found in the basic nature of Westerners. Most, except for the original inhabitants, have traveled from other lands to live in the West. These immigrants tended to be creative people, free thinkers, innovators. As the past two centuries have shown, development in the West has brought about thousands of inventions that have transformed the way we live. We value new ideas and hold onto old ideas only to the extent that those ideas are still helpful. But a society that values new ideas must also have reliable ways to evaluate each idea as it comes. We need more than opinion. We need recognized methods that will help us determine whether that idea should be welcomed or rejected.

The West does not have a long history. We know very little about the kind of traditional learning that you are simply supposed to accept because it has built in value. Instead, we construct knowledge for ourselves by introducing new concepts, evaluating them, and adding everything we finally accept to the knowledge we already have. Even then, something we accepted twenty years ago may, through the process of critical thinking, be rejected today if there is no good reason for keeping it.

The West is losing its concept of truth defined as something that everyone recognizes. Postmodernism argues that there are many truths, because each of us has his or her own view of life. If truth that we can agree upon is difficult to find (though I believe it still exists), then we need critical thinking as a means of evaluating—with evidence—various points of view in order to determine which is the most convincing.

If you have come from an educational system in which critical thinking was not taught to students or encouraged among them, then you will experience struggles in the classroom and in the essays you write. Developing the skills of critical thinking is of utmost importance. In the West, we value the ability to analyze much more than we value the ability to memorize.

But how do you learn critical thinking?

- Your institution may offer a course in critical thinking or in logic.

- There may be a seminar in critical thinking offered in your city.

- There are several good books on critical thinking available, some of them with practice exercises.

- The Internet has many valuable sites related to critical thinking. Here are a few addresses:

**http://www.philosophy.unimelb.edu.au/reason/critical/**
**http://sorrel.humboldt.edu/~act/**—a tutorial you can take
**http://www.coping.org/adultlink/think.htm**—a guide to several tutorials

*Note: Over time, some of the above Internet addresses may change. If you are looking for other sites, do a google.com search on "critical thinking."*

- Begin practicing critical thinking skills yourself. If you have been in the habit of simply accepting information as it is given to you, begin evaluating it in your own mind. Ask yourself things like this:

  - How reliable is the source of this information?

  - How much does this information agree with other things I know?

  - Is there a reason I should be suspicious about this information?

  - Is there other information that would contradict it?

  - Are there parts of the information that are missing or are stated incorrectly?

  - How much evidence supports this information, and how reliable is that evidence?

You do not have to become negative and challenge everything you hear. But you must learn to be discerning, never accepting what you hear until you have evaluated it.

## Taking Notes

As a student from another country, you will find that recording what you are learning is a challenge. Some students ask permission actually to tape record their classes, but there are professors who do not allow it, and you may not have time to listen to your recordings later in the day. Thus you are left with note taking as the best method to keep a record of what happened in the classroom.

As you will discover, professors in the West do not just lecture. They include classroom discussions, small group discussions, seminars and other teaching methods that do not make note taking easy. You will need to remember that the gaining of knowledge is only one part of Western education. In the classroom, the professor is also teaching you how to use your knowledge in critical thinking situations. Never forget that Westerners value knowledge only to the extent that it is useful. This means that your education will have to include training in *using*, not just memorizing, information.

But there will be times in most class sessions when the professor will simply be lecturing—sharing knowledge with students. Unless you have a perfect memory, you will need to take notes in order to retain what you have heard. This is not easy for most students, but you face the additional challenge of taking notes from someone who has a different national language and culture from your own. Simply understanding what you are hearing is enough of a challenge. But you must record it as well.

Here are some suggestions for developing your note-taking skills:

- Continue to work on your English listening and speaking skills.

- Begin your notes for each class on a new page in your notebook. At the top, record the name of the course, the date, and (if you know it) the topic of that day's class. Number your note pages so that they will always be kept in order.

- Listen very carefully to each professor's method of presentation. Does s/he use many words to say everything or does s/he use few words but say a lot? Does s/he use slang and colloquial expressions or speak in standard English? Long sentences or short ones? Complicated language or simple words? Just listening for a while can help you begin to understand the way your professor communicates.

---

NOTE: From this point, I will be using the term **s/he** as a short way of saying "she or he."

---

- Recognize that everyone who speaks uses what are called "key propositions." These are important sentences that tell you what the professor really believes or really wants to tell you. The rest of what s/he says is introduction, illustration or evidence. The rule is to *listen for key propositions and write them down.*

- Use point form as much as possible. You don't need full sentences. Develop abbreviations for common words, for example, &=and, w/o=without, three dots in a triangle=therefore, e.g.=for example, and so on. As much as possible, try to record a lot of information without having to write a lot. Abbreviate everything you can.

  For example, the professor may say something like: "There have been several challenges to Lynn White's article over the past few years. Some have accused him of misunderstanding the teaching of Genesis. Others have said that it is wrong to accuse the whole Judeo-Christian tradition for the misinterpretations of a few people. Clearly the debate is far from over, but White may not be as justified as he thinks he is." Using short form and listening for key propositions, you might write in your notes: **Some disagree with White, e.g. he misunderstood Genesis or blamed whole religion for wrong views of a few. Prof says White could be wrong.**

- You will not be able to record everything your professor says, but it's better to record too much than to record too little. Try to put down all the key propositions and then anything else that seems important. If you have time right after class, go over your notes and record anything else you remember.

- If there was anything you really did not understand, either ask the professor during class to explain it or go to the professor after class. If the professor is not available, ask a fellow student. Then record in your notes what you have learned.

- In the evening after each day in which you took notes, read them over several times. We tend to forget the most within 24 hours after we hear something. By reviewing your notes just a few hours after you made them, you help yourself to/put the information into your long term memory.

- There are a number of websites that can help you with further suggestions on taking notes. Here are two of them:

  **http://www.utexas.edu/student/utlc/makinggrade/ inclassnotes.html**
  **http://www.byu.edu/ccc/learning/note-tak.shtml—describes the famous Cornell system for taking notes, a helpful method for most class situations.**

  *Note: Over time, some of the above Internet addresses may change. If you are looking for other sites, do a google.com search on "note taking."*

## Computer/Internet Abilities

If you do not already have a computer and Internet connection that are easily available to you, it will become increasingly important that you get one. Whether you need to prepare a written assignment, do research, communicate with your professor by e-mail, or take an online course, a computer properly connected to the Internet is a must.

If you do not already have basic computer skills and some knowledge of Internet and e-mail, take a short study course to get you started. Your Student Services department can likely direct you to the proper kind of training. The days of handwritten assignments and research done only within a library are over. Now you need access to the whole world of information and the technology as well as the tools to produce assignments that please your professors, whose eyes are already strained from reading poorly produced essays in the past.

There are more skills that you will need, but we will deal with these as we come to them in the following chapters.

# 3

# *The Classroom—New Ways of Learning*

When you first enter a Western classroom, you might find it very familiar—a room full of desks or tables with a podium at the front, a blackboard or whiteboard, and an overhead projector. If you look at the ceiling or at the back of the class, you may see another projector that allows students to view videos, DVDs or computer displays. Other than this last equipment, you've seen everything before.

But the sense of familiarity will end when your fellow students enter the room. The first thing you will notice is that they seem very casual about being in class. They will talk, joke, perhaps move from seat to seat. Some will come late. Most of them show no sense of anxiety about what they may face in the coming class. They seem to have the same sort of behavior you would expect from people attending a concert or sports event. You will wonder why they are so disrespectful, and why they seem not at all worried that their professor will be displeased with their casual attitude.

You will likely discover, to your amazement, that many professors share the same sort of casual approach to the classroom as their students do. A few might be stern and demanding, but most will be friendly and informal. It might almost seem as if they want to be on an equal level with their students rather than above their students, as the professors in your homeland are.

Let us see if we can understand what is happening here.

# Chaos in the Classroom?

You wonder why neither students nor faculty seems to take Western education as seriously as they should. Education is a serious thing, after all. Yet the classroom in this new country seems to be a place of informality and lack of structure. When the professor comes into the room, most students do not even acknowledge him or her. They don't stop discussing with one another, and it is the professor who has to call them to attention. Even then, the professor does not seem upset with the lack of respect. During the class, you notice one student chewing gum, another looking out the window, and still another drinking from a can of Coke. The professor says nothing about any of this behavior.

If you look closer, however, you will see that education is going on despite the feeling that the class appears disorganized. It's just a different kind of education, one that goes two ways rather than one. What do I mean by that? I mean that in Western education, the students are active participants. They are not there just to absorb information but to *work with* information by responding to it, even questioning or criticizing it. The professor asks questions to draw out responses from students (something that can be difficult when the class is held just after lunch hour and students are sleepy). The professor, as well, will likely encourage active participation by calling for discussion or assigning various students to give presentations.

The main difference between the Western classroom and the type of education you may be used to is that, in the Western classroom, the student is expected to be an active learner, deeply involved in interaction with what is being taught. Thus, if the topic of the class is the Causes of World War I, the professor may lecture about several possible causes and then move the class into a discussion of them. S/he may ask, "Are any of the suggested causes unlikely or lacking evidence? Of many suggested causes, which are the most significant? Are there other possible causes that have not yet been suggested?" And so on.

You are actually familiar with this process already. The difference is that it was likely your professor who raised such issues and then responded to them before finally expressing his/her own solution. It was not the task of the student to debate these things. The issues in a controversy were debated, but only by the professor. The significant difference in the West is that *the students are expected to be part of the debate and to make their own contribution to it.* In most cases, the professor does not tell them what to believe. That conclusion is up to the student

Thus what you see as chaos is actually active learning. To be sure, there are a few students who are lazy and careless. There are a few professors who are more concerned about their research than their teaching skills. But most of what you see as disorganized activity is actually an exercise in active learning that invites students to be involved with what they are hearing from the professor—to work with it, evaluate it, discuss it, debate about it.

Here is a quotation from a syllabus for a course on American Folk History that illustrates what many Western professors are looking for in their classes:

> *"Especially in a class of this size, I look forward to the free, sometimes heated, intellectual exchange generated by our readings and our community of interest in understanding the American folk."*
>
> —Michael Steiner, **http://hss.fullerton.edu/amst/courses/ms-amst440.html** [accessed October 20, 2002]

There it is: "Free, sometimes heated [that is, emotional] intellectual exchange," in which ideas are thrown around the room, people react, discussion happens, emotions stir, and the result is a deeper understanding of the subject than the professor could have provided by himself or herself.

When professor and student interact in this kind of learning experience, some of the difference in rank between them tends to disappear. You will see that professors and students act more like friends than masters and disciples. Professors may let students address them by their first names. There may be sharp differences of opinion between them, with students criticizing the views of professors and professors criticizing the views of students. This is not disrespect in most cases. It is simply a different approach to the relationship between teacher and pupil.

But don't Westerners honor their professors? Yes, they do, but the honor must be earned. It is not automatically given. Rather, as students observe professors doing their work well, professors gain more and more honor. True, professors must always be respected, and rudeness is not allowed from students or professors, but those who teach well gain more honor.

## Question and Answer

Even when a professor is lecturing, there will be times when s/he will ask what are called "leading questions," questions intended to start discussion on a topic. The philosophy behind leading questions is that students learn better if they are actively involved in the process of learning rather than just sitting and listening. The professor may, as well, want to teach some of the skills of critical thinking by having the students actually do it.

Leading questions are risky both for the professor and for the student. In undergraduate classes in particular, students often simply stare back at the professor, none of them willing to suggest an answer. This leaves the professor having to wait awkwardly and then answer the question him/herself instead of the students doing it. As an alternative to this, the professor may "call on" a student, actually directing the question to one person in the class who will then either have to answer it or look foolish. In graduate level classes, the level of interaction is much higher, and professors tend not to need to call on one student

In my experience, international students often avoid answering leading questions because they fear their English is not good enough to make the answer clear or because they struggle with understanding the question. Another reason is not quite as obvious: international students may not be used to answering questions at all unless there is a single answer. For example, if you are asked, "What is the capital of South

Korea?" you can easily give a response because the answer is based on memory. Unfortunately, leading questions in Western classrooms often depend on more than memory. Instead of asking, "What is the capital of South Korea?" the professor may ask a question like, "Why do you think South Korea recovered so quickly from the Asian financial crisis of 1999?" The response to this requires analysis and evaluation. It demands that you gather all the facts together in your mind and use them as tools to work out a solution to a problem. You may never have had to answer such questions before.

One way to save yourself embarrassment is simply never to answer leading questions. But what if the professor calls on you? If that happens, the worst thing you can do is just sit there in silence while the seconds tick by. If you think you know the answer, say it. You might be wrong, and that might make you uncomfortable, but it's better to try than to avoid the problem. If you truly don't know, simply say, "I'm sorry. I don't know."

But what if the professor never calls on you? Should you always remain silent? The answer is "no." If you avoid answering leading questions, you will miss the opportunity to get all the benefit out of the class that you could. It takes a lot of courage to respond to a question without being called on, especially when there is a risk that you could be wrong. But you've already shown you have courage. Ask yourself, will the embarrassment kill you if you are wrong?

## *Imagine*

PROFESSOR: Let's return the Lynn White's argument. He accuses the Judeo-Christian heritage with being a strong force in the current environmental crisis. What do you think his most significant evidence is? [a leading question—he looks out at the class].

YOU: He says the Bible tells us to have dominion over nature [an easy answer because you memorized the main features of White's article].

PROFESSOR: Good. Now [still looking at you] do you think, first of all, that the Bible does indeed encourage environmental abuse, and, second, that those in the Judeo-Christian heritage have used the dominion teaching as an excuse for damaging the environment? *(Now you really have a really challenge. Not only has the professor asked you to do critical thinking, but s/he has given you two questions.)*

YOU: What was the first question?

PROFESSOR: Does the Bible encourage environmental abuse?

YOU: I don't think so.

PROFESSOR: Why?

YOU: It's the Bible. They call it "the good book."

PROFESSOR: That's not evidence of anything.

YOU: [thinking deeply] If the Bible says God created the world, why would it encourage people to destroy it?

PROFESSOR: Good. Now, do you think those in the Judeo-Christian heritage have used the dominion teaching as an excuse to abuse the earth?

YOU: I'm sorry. I really don't know.

PROFESSOR: Anyone else? [looking around the class].

You have survived. True, you didn't know the answer to the last question, but you did all right on the earlier one. In the process, you have been challenged to think, and you've likely learned something of value.

## Group Discussions

Your professor may break the class up into small groups to discuss an issue so you can come back to the larger group with insights that will help the class move toward a solution. In a large class, you may even have scheduled discussion times in smaller groups of 12 to 20 students (sometimes called a *tutorial*). You may be given a group assignment in which each member of the group must contribute to a final presentation.

The common element in all of these is discussion, and it's a difficult situation for most international students. Why?

- If your training in English has focused more on written than spoken English, you will find that your listening skills seem less advanced in group discussion with other students than they were in the classroom when your professor was giving a lecture. This is because a professor tends to choose words more carefully and use more standard English. Your fellow students are more likely to use the language of everyday speech, which is full of colloquial expressions.

  To deal with this problem, you need to concentrate on your listening ability, trying to make sense of the sentences being spoken by using the words you do understand to help you fill in the gaps of the words you didn't understand. Don't be afraid to say, "Excuse me, I missed what you just said," or even to say to the whole group, "I'm still learning English. Do you think you could speak a bit more slowly?" Most students will be happy to help you. It's very important to keep working on your listening skills. Review the information in Chapter Two related to doing this.

- Not only are you trying to understand, but you are also expected to use the information you already have to evaluate issues, arguments, and evidence, in order to solve problems. This is where critical thinking skills come in. Critical thinking can be developed only through training and practice. Avoid the temptation to sit quietly and let everyone else speak. The best way to advance in group discussion is to make sure you actually do some of the discussing. You have an advantage—a good memory. This will help you keep the facts available in your mind as you answer those difficult questions that will come. Keep working on your critical thinking skills.

Group discussions and group projects are intended to teach the skills not just of critical thinking but of collaboration. What is "collaboration?" It is the ability of a group to use the skills of each member to create a solution that is better than the solution that any of the members could have found on their own. Group skills are important to most subject areas, because groups have great power to increase the abilities of each member, as if the group members had merged together to become like one super person with advanced skills.

In order for you to benefit from the group experience and for the group to benefit from your membership in it, you need to participate in everything, despite your hesitation to do so. Western education values the powers of collaboration. The more you get involved with the others in your group, the more you will learn about collaboration. Gather together all your courage and speak out in every group you're involved with.

Be careful, though. Once you begin speaking out in groups, you may find you like it a lot. You must remember, however, that everyone in the group needs to participate. If there are ten people in the group, be sure you are speaking no more than 10% of the time.

What do you, a student from another country, have to contribute to a discussion group?

- A perspective different from those of other students in the group. You come from a another culture that may provide special insights to the problems your group is trying to deal with. If your culture has something positive to say to a problem, never hesitate to speak it.

- Your ability to memorize will probably be stronger than that of other members of your group. Contribute information as you notice others in the class struggling to remember.

- The fact that you are part of the group means that you do have a contribution to make. Do not let yourself feel like a second-class member. Membership gives you the privilege of having a voice in what the group accomplishes.

# Class Presentations

In some classes, you will be asked to make an individual or group presentation to the rest of the class. This will seem like the worst kind of assignment, an invitation to humiliate yourself in public. But the first thing you need to do when you learn that you are going to have to do a presentation, is to control the panic that you feel. Recognize the following:

- Most people have a fear of public speaking. Thus your fear is not unusual. Your fellow class members share in that emotion, even if they were born in the West.

- The better you are prepared for a presentation, the more confidence you will have and the less risk there will be of humiliation.

Why would a professor, who is paid to teach you, want you to take his teaching time to make a presentation? That is a good question. Indeed, there may be some professors who like to do less preparation of their own lectures and thus use student presentations as a way of avoiding teaching. But that is rare. In most cases, the professor has a clear plan in asking you to make a presentation:

- S/he wants to see evidence that you understand and are able to work with the things you are learning in class. The expectation is that you will use critical thinking to present a topic in such a way that you resolve an issue or solve a problem.

- S/he may see this as a way to improve your public speaking skills, something most universities want you to do throughout your program.

- S/he may want to see how well you "think on your feet," that is, explain various points without a lot of preparation. True, you will prepare and perhaps even memorize your presentation. But there will also be time for the professor and your fellow students to question you about the information you have presented.

How does an international student survive a class presentation? The first thing you need to do is prepare very well. Write the whole presentation out. Memorize important parts of it. Prepare visual aids: If you have PowerPoint skills, prepare a PowerPoint presentation. Otherwise, prepare overheads.

Second, practice doing your entire presentation several times before you actually do it in class. Pay attention to the parts where you are forgetting important information, stumbling over what you are saying or feeling that your presentation is unclear. Then correct those things. Play close attention to time. If the professor wants you to complete the presentation in 15 minutes, make sure it takes 12 to 15 minutes to complete, no more, no less. If you have a good friend who can listen to the presentation and provide helpful criticism, you can identify problems that you have overlooked.

Keep your presentation simple. Follow exactly the instructions your professor gave you. Avoid big words and long sentences. Use clear logic in presenting your information so your outline makes sense and everyone who hears you will have good understanding. Do not try to impress the class with complexity or over use of technology. It is better to have a clear but less exciting presentation than to create something that everyone remembers as difficult to understand.

*More guidance on doing presentations will be found in Chapter 7.*

## Labs

Many science courses, as well as courses in geography, languages and some other subjects, have a lab (short for "laboratory") requirement that is generally taken outside of the normal classroom hours. Labs are intended to provide you with practical and "hands on" experience in the things you are learning in class. For example, a chemistry class may be covering a certain type of chemical reaction. In the lab, you will follow instructions to use real chemicals and create the same reaction. A language lab will give you conversation practice in the language you are studying.

The keys to succeeding in lab situations are three:

- Read and be very familiar with all instructions you are given in advance, so that you can enter the lab as prepared as possible. Labs tend to require you to move through procedures quickly. If you are not prepared, you will likely fall behind.

- Follow instructions exactly. Do not assume that the instructions are just suggestions and that you can use your own methods. You will be told what you need to do. Stay very closely within the boundaries of the instructions you are given.

- If you do not understand what you need to do, ask the person who is directing your lab. Do not simply go ahead and hope you will do it right. In fact, most directors of labs expect you to ask if something is not clear.

## Class Attendance

Some of your fellow students may tell you that class attendance is not required, so it's all right to skip a few classes during the semester. That may be true for some students, but as an international student struggling with a new method of education, you can't afford to miss anything. Attend every class. Try to be early. Listen attentively. Record as many notes as you can. Enter discussion often. Try to get as much benefit from each class as you possibly can.

## Mediated Learning and the Virtual Campus

Classrooms are changing. Where once the only technology was an overhead projector, you now could find video recording and projection, computer projection, smart screens, and so on. With such resources, the classroom becomes much "bigger," because it opens access to the world of images, sound, and Internet. The professor can do a PowerPoint demonstration, show you a clip of a movie, take you to a website, or videotape your class presentation.

All of this is called "mediated learning," because the technology acts as a "mediator" between the professor and you so that the professor's ideas and information can be presented in more powerful forms. The use of such technology is growing year by year, often making the professor only one element in the learning experience.

You may be feeling impatient about the use of technology, because a professor simply lecturing can usually deliver much more information in an hour than he or she can when technology is used, and it's a much simpler process. But recognize that, although a video clip or Power-Point demonstration may deliver less actual information, it can help you understand and remember more of what you are being taught. When you both see and hear information, your knowledge gains depth, and becomes real in your mind, so that it is something more to you than words in a notebook.

If you are not comfortable with technology—computers, video, and so on—you need to do everything you can to gain technological skills. Take a computer course. Learn how to operate a DVD player. You can think you are able to resist technology, but it is here to stay, and you will need it in most aspects of your life and career. The sooner you get up to date, the better.

Many universities are now developing "virtual campuses." At the beginning, these were Internet programs and sites that helped deliver online courses that had no need of a classroom. Now regular courses are making use of websites where you will find your syllabus, assignments, additional reading, even online projects, discussion sessions, quizzes and examinations. Professors may use the class website to make announcements, provide links to web sites that give you further information about things you have been studying in class, or leave instructions about the proper format for research projects.

The most important thing you need to do if your course has its own Internet site is to make sure that you look at the site at least once a day. Check if there are any announcements or updates, and see what will be covered in the next class. Make sure you are not caught by surprise because you failed to keep up to date with what was posted on the class site.

## Online Courses

Online courses are growing in popularity. Imagine not having to go to a classroom, not having to follow a rigid schedule, and being able to turn in an assignment from your home by e-mail at 2:00 in the morning. No wonder many students see clear advantages to doing courses online by using a computer instead of going to a classroom.

International students may find even more of an advantage. In the classroom, they often misunderstand spoken English because it goes too fast. With an online course, they can read the English slowly and even look up unfamiliar words in a dictionary. In the classroom, they may have to answer questions or be involved in discussion. With an online course, even if there is an online discussion session, they can type carefully, taking time to make sure the words are correct.

But, as an international student, you need to be cautious about online courses for a number of reasons:

- Despite what many educators tell us, online courses sometimes do not teach as much content as live courses.

- Online courses are all right as long as you understand the information or assignments you are being given. But if you do not understand something, it can be harder to reach the professor for an explanation than in a live course.

- Online courses are lonely. You work on them by yourself. Some students find this difficult, or they feel like they are not really becoming familiar with the information in the course, because they are unable to discuss course material with others.

- Online courses require self-discipline. The fact that there is not as much of a schedule means that you will have to create your own schedule in order to make sure your assignments are completed in time.

Here are some suggestions to follow if you decide to take an online course. These come from my own experience with leading international students in such courses:

- When you first enter the Internet site where the course is to be found, spend an hour or so looking at everything in the course. Make sure you understand the software that controls the site. Concentrate especially on what assignments will be required and what deadlines are set. Try to estimate how long each assignment will take you and write down the number of hours you have estimated. Then add at least 50% more. That is, if you thought a certain assignment would take you 4 hours to complete, add 2 more hours and estimate that it will take you 6 hours.

- To set up a schedule for yourself, use whatever deadlines you are given as well as your own estimates of time needed to do each assignment. Your schedule should give you a good idea of how many hours per week you will need to spend. Then you should write down actual periods of time during the week when you will work on the course (for example, Monday 1:00-2:30; Tuesday 9:00-10:00 and so on), making sure that you schedule two or three hours more than you will actually need.

- Don't forget that you have other courses and responsibilities. Make sure that you have scheduled sufficient time to do them as well.

- Never, never leave an online course to the last half of the semester, hoping that you will have time to complete it then. The only way to do an online course safely is to spend the same amount of time on it each week from the first day of the course until the last.

- Read instructions very carefully. You do not have a professor close at hand to explain them to you. If any instruction is unclear to you, contact the supervisor of the course and ask for an explanation. You, and only you, are responsible to read instructions correctly.

- If possible, turn in your assignments one at a time as you complete them. In this way, if you are making a mistake in the way you are doing something, the professor can correct you before you turn in more assignments that also have errors in them.

- Pay close attention to any corrections or instructions a professor makes on the assignment you have submitted. What the professor is telling you is intended to be part of the teaching process.

- Do not turn assignments in late. If the first one is late, you will now have the responsibility to turn in that assignment while at the same time struggling to get the second assignment in on time. It's likely the second will be late as well, then the third, and so on.

- If the professor schedules online "chat" or discussion sessions, when class members interact on particular issues, be very sure you are involved in each one of them. You may not think you have a lot to contribute, but try to contribute something.

Classrooms in the West are different from what you have known. Technology is making them even more different than they were a few years ago. Do not panic. Other international students before you have learned to do well in classes that at first looked like dangerous chaos. In time, you will find that you appreciate the "free and sometimes heated" exchange of ideas. In time, even mediated classrooms and online courses will seem familiar to you.

# 4

## *The Classroom—Syllabus, Notes and Assignments*

We've looked at the "dynamic" side of classroom life—the lectures, the questions and answers, the discussions, and so on. But there is also another side—the written side—that needs careful attention.

### The Syllabus

At the beginning of almost every course you take, you will receive a syllabus, a statement of what the course will contain and what it will require. Your syllabus may be printed on paper or be found online, but it will be a document that should never be very far from your thoughts.

Did you know that a syllabus is actually a contract? By receiving it, you enter into an agreement with your professor and your university. The professor promises to provide you with education as described in the syllabus, and you agree to provide the professor with attendance and the assignments you are asked to do. If your professor does not bring you the education that was promised, you have the right to protest to the university. If you do not complete the assignments as laid out in the syllabus, the professor has the right to give you a low mark or even a failure.

The syllabus is the roadmap for the course you are taking, the agenda, the central document. So what, exactly, is in it? Formats for syllabi (the plural form of "syllabus") vary greatly. Some are short, perhaps only a page long. Others are much longer. There are some common features, however:

- A brief description of the course content.

- A statement of the objectives of the course—what the professor wants you to learn.

- A statement about required and optional textbooks and reading materials.

- An outline of the course. (This is not always provided.)

- A list of assignments that you must complete.

The professor may also include special instructions to help you accomplish your assignments, as well as a description of how grading will be done, warnings about late assignments, warnings about plagiarism, and so on.

So what do you do with a syllabus? ***Read it.*** Read it often and be very familiar with it. If there are parts of it you do not understand, ask your professor early in the semester to explain those parts for you. Let's consider each section as you might find it in a typical syllabus:

- Course Content—This short statement, often called a "course description," is a bit like an advertisement for the course. It is the promise of what the major emphases of the course will be.

- Course Objectives—The objectives tell you what the professor intends to be the result if you take the course. Here the professor will describe the main things you are supposed to learn and indicated how the course is going to change you or change the way you think.

- Textbook(s) and Readings—Reading in any course is likely going to take you a long time. This section of the syllabus is important to you, because it tells you what you will need to read. The first thing you need to do is to be sure that you have access to all the reading materials. If you have the money and the reading materials are available for sale, it is best to buy them so that you have them when you want them. Otherwise, try to sign them out from the library, taking note of the due date so that you will have the reading done before you have to return them. They may be on special reserve that allows you to take them out for only short periods of time—a few hours or one to three days.

Next you need to evaluate the reading you are asked to do. How much of it is required and how much is optional? In general, students never do optional reading unless they have a great deal of extra time. Once you have discovered what you are expected to read, count the total number of pages, and take a few minutes to read 5-10 pages of each book or article so that you can determine what is an average reading time per page. If it takes 1.5 minutes to read one page, it will take 900 minutes (= 15 hours) to read 600 pages. Later, when you do your assignment schedule (see below), you can determine how many minutes per day need to be devoted to reading.

What I have to say now will not make your professor happy, but it is you who have to live in a real world with many demands upon your time. When you get to the portion of your syllabus dealing with reading, be sure you discover what marks you will receive for completing it. Generally this will be 5—15% of the total course grade. Do you need to submit reading reports? A journal? If not, you may want to consider the possibility that reading will be less of a priority—you will do it if you have time, but you might not do all of it. Think carefully about this decision though.

Try to get the reading done, but if it is not worth a significant percentage of your grade, it will likely be the first assignment to leave undone. In some cases, the professor wants you to do reading in stages as you go through the semester, so that there is a reading assignment to be completed before you come to each class. Even if the grade is not high for this, you may have to take it more seriously, because the reading you do will help you perform better in the classroom.

A speed reading course may be helpful to you, but speed reading only works well if your level of English understanding is good. If it is not, you will find that your reading slows anyway as you spend time thinking about what the words and sentences actually mean.

- Course Outline—While not always provided, a course outline can help you visualize where the course is going in relation to the reading and assignments you are completing. Some professors will even indicate what will be covered in each class session. All such information helps you to plan properly throughout the course.

- Course Assignments—We will deal with assignments in much more detail below. Occasionally a professor will not list the assignments in the syllabus but will promise to tell the class later what will be expected. *This is not a good procedure at all,* because it means you can't plan your work through the semester. A professor like this will probably surprise you in mid semester with a big assignment just when you have other projects due. If you are in a course that has no assignments, or not all of the assignments are listed in the syllabus, try to transfer to another section taught by someone else. If you cannot do this, go to the professor and tell him/her that as an international student who has difficulty with assignments, you need to plan your time well from the beginning of the semester. Have the courage to ask the professor to provide you with a printed statement of what assignments will be required for the whole semester.

## Class Notes

We discussed note-taking briefly in an earlier chapter. Here we need to look at what your notes are supposed to accomplish and what you need to do to organize and make best use of them.

Your class notes are your main record of the content of the course you are taking. They are like the photographs or videos you may have kept from your childhood. When you look at those visual images later in life, they help preserve your memories of childhood like nothing else could do. In the same way, the notes you take in class help you to make firm and concrete memories of what happened in the class. Those who take only a few notes and trust their memories either have very, very good memories, or they really do not care if much of their learning experience is not preserved.

What should your notes record?

- The main questions—Every course involves discovering answers to questions, whether you are studying mathematics or philosophy. Your professor will raise questions, issues, or problems. So will your discussion group if there is one. You need to keep a record of every question and of the solutions that were suggested.

- Important information that serves as background or answers to questions—Take note of information the professor emphasizes. Always write down anything that the professor indicates is a solution or is important to know. You can't record everything, but your notes should be a summary of the main things the professor said. Similarly, within discussion groups, anything that appears to be valuable information should be noted.

  Pay special attention to answers to questions. You may discover that there are several possible answers. Note down each one that you hear suggested, recognizing that the professor might eventually lead the class to accept one of them, but alternatively, s/he might expect each student to reach his/her own conclusion.

- Evidence—In the Western classroom, simply recording facts will not be enough. At the end of the course, when you take exams, you will find that you are being tested, not just on what you know but on how well you can think through problems and find solutions. Your professor during a class session will raise question, suggests several possible answers, and then lead the class through evaluation of evidence. The professor and class will discuss possible solutions. As far as your notes are concerned, the professor's method of solving the problem as well as the evidence s/he refers to need to be recorded in full. Later you will have a record of models for solving problems, in case you are asked problem-solving questions on an exam.

If you include in your notes the evidence the professor discusses, paying attention to the ways in which the evidence helps you to reach an answer, you will have the whole thing—question, evidence, and solution—there in your notes when you are done.

## Computers and Notes

Using a notebook computer or a Palm to record notes may be a good idea, but you need to think through whether or not this method is better than simply recording notes on paper. Do you type faster than you write? Can you be sure you will have a secure power source through the whole class? Do you want to carry your computer with you through the day or is it too bulky? Are you prepared to back up your notes in case you lose your data? Are you aware that notebook computers and Palms get stolen regularly, and are you able to keep your machine secure? Finally, are there real advantages to using high technology instead of paper and ink? If the advantages are few, you might as well use and pen and paper.

## Your Notes after Class

If you don't make proper use of your notes once you have taken them, they will do you very little good. Each evening, take 15 minutes to put that day's date on each set of notes you took, then read over the notes of the day. On the weekend, read over all your notes for the past week. What you are trying to do is to put your notes into your long-term memory. The chances are that your memory is good because you have been trained to use it all your life.

But you must do a lot more than memorize your notes. You must use your notes as a means to learn how to solve problems with evidence. The midterm or final examination might well have a question like: "Present several reasons why it is likely that Lynn White overstated his case in blaming the Judeo-Christian philosophies for the environmental crisis." You are training yourself now how to think within the subject area you are studying, and your notes are a guide to the way this was done in the classroom. Studying your professor's methods of dealing with controversy and issues is important. Your notes should be a useful record of those methods.

## Assignments

In chapters that follow, we will be considering the various kinds of assignments you may encounter. Right now, however, we need to look at how to organize your *assignment schedule.*

If you can get to an office supply store, you will find that it has many kinds of appointment calendars for sale. The kind you will be most interested is a large one on one sheet that allows you to see 6-12 months all at once, each day indicated as a square on which you can write. The purpose of such a calendar will be to plot out all of your assignment due dates for each course you are taking for the semester. You might want to get a multi-color set of fine point markers as well, so that you can reserve a single color for each course.

Using the due dates in your syllabus, write the course number and a short title for each assignment on the proper date squares in your calendar. When you are done, you will have a schedule for all your due dates for the semester.

But this is only the beginning. Students who only pay attention to due dates regularly turn in late assignments. Why? Because they forget that some assignments take much longer than others. Since we tend to start our projects only when the due date is close, more difficult assignments can end up not being done on time. The next step you need to complete is to develop a *schedule based on start dates.* This can be done in a paper notebook or a computer file.

First look at each assignment and estimate how long it will take you to complete. This is not easy to do. Here are some clues that can help you:

- Look at the grades that are indicated for each assignment. A term essay that is worth 30% of your total mark for the course will likely take about one-third of all the time you have to do assignments in the course. I usually estimate that doing all a course's assignments takes 2 hours for every hour in class. Thus, if you have 36 class hours, you will likely need 72 hours to complete your assignments. Thirty percent of 72 is about 22 hours. Be careful, though. Reading assignments usually take a lot of time but often give you few marks.

- Assignments on subjects with which you are familiar with will likely take less time to do than assignments you have never encountered before.

- Assignments that require research take longer than assignments that just ask you to interact with material you've studied in class.

- You need to schedule time to prepare for quizzes and examinations beyond the other assignments. Here, the percentage of your grade that an exam is worth is a good guide for how much time you should spend preparing.

Suppose, then, that you have a research paper due on November 19. You believe it will take you about 22 hours to complete. If you spent one hour per day on it, you should likely start working on it on October 29. This, of course, assumes that you actually will spend one hour per day on it and that you won't get sick or have some emergency that prevents you from meeting your schedule. What I suggest is that you allow more time. Instead of starting on October 29, start on October 23.

This is where scheduling assignments becomes complicated: If you have several courses, all with assignments, you are going to have to create a master list of start dates so that you can schedule all of them. It might look something like this:

**Date**                    **Assignment**

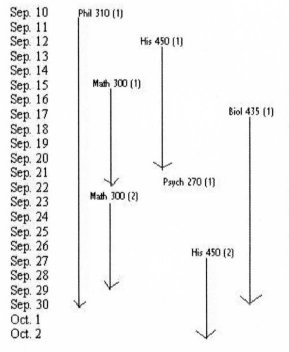

Just look across horizontally for each date, and you will see what projects you are working on and how many total hours you will need to spend that day. For example, on September 19, you have one hour of Phil 310, one hour of Math 300, one hour of His 450, and one hour of Biol 435.

Another way to do the same thing is this:

Sep. 10     Phil 320 (1) one hour per day to Sep 30
Sep. 11
Sep. 12     His 450 (1) half hour per day to Sep. 21
Sep. 13
Sep. 14
Sep. 15     Math 300 (1) one hour per day to Sep. 22
Sep. 16

Sep. 17    Biol 435 (1) half hour per day to Sep. 30
Sep. 18
Sep. 19
Sep. 20
Sep. 21
Sep. 22    Psych 270 (1) half hour only on Sep. 22
Sep. 23    Math. 300 (2) one hour per day to Sep. 29
Sep. 24
Sep. 25
Sep. 26
Sep. 27    His 450(2) half hour per day to Oct. 2
Sep. 28
Sep. 29
Sep. 30
Oct. 1
Oct. 2

Or do it with a calendar:

| Sunday | Monday | Tuesday | Wednesday | Thursday | Friday | Saturday |
|---|---|---|---|---|---|---|
| 10<br>Ph 320(1) 1hr | 11<br>Ph 320(1) 1hr | 12<br>Ph 320(1) 1hr<br>His 450(1) ½ | 13<br>Ph 320(1) 1hr<br>His 450(1) ½ | 14<br>Ph 320(1) 1hr<br>His 450(1) ½ | 15<br>Ph 320(1) 1hr<br>His 450(1) ½ | 16<br>Ph 320(1) 1hr<br>His 450(1) ½<br>Mth 300(1) 1 |
| 17<br>Ph 320(1) 1hr<br>His 450(1) ½<br>Mth 300(1) 1 | 18<br>Ph 320(1) 1hr<br>His 450(1) ½<br>Mth 300(1) 1<br>Bio 435(1) ½ | 19<br>Ph 320(1) 1hr<br>His 450(1) ½<br>Mth 300(1) 1<br>Bio 435(1) ½ | 20<br>Ph 320(1) 1hr<br>His 450(1) ½<br>Mth 300(1) 1<br>Bio 435(1) ½ | 21<br>Ph 320(1) 1hr<br>His450(1) end<br>Mth 300(1) 1<br>Bio 435(1) ½ | 22<br>Ph 320(1) 1hr<br>Mth300(1) end<br>Bio 435(1) ½<br>Psy 270(1) ½ | 23<br>Ph 320(1) 1hr<br>His 450(1) ½<br>Mth 300(2) 1 |
| 24<br>Ph 320(1) 1hr<br>Bio 435(1) ½<br>Mth 300(2) 1 | 25<br>Ph 320(1) 1hr<br>Bio 435(1) ½<br>Mth 300(2) 1 | 26<br>Ph 320(1) 1hr<br>Bio 435(1) ½<br>Mth 300(2) 1 | 27<br>Ph 320(1) 1hr<br>Bio 435(1) ½<br>Mth 300(2) 1<br>His 450(2) ½ | 28<br>Ph 320(1) 1hr<br>Bio 435(1) ½<br>Mth 300(2) 1<br>His 450 (2) ½ | 29<br>Ph 320(1) 1hr<br>Bio 435(1) ½<br>Mth300(2) end<br>His 450 (2) ½ | 30<br>Ph 320(1) end<br>Bio 435(1) ½<br>His 450 (2) ½ |

The calendar method, in fact, is probably the best way to tell you what to work on each day and how much work you will need to do. If one day has too much work in it, you may be able to adjust the schedule somewhat to even out the work through your week.

Regardless of how you schedule it, you need to do the difficult work of planning the whole semester so that you have time to complete everything. But there are some possible problems to deal with:

- What if you have several assignments due the same day? When you plan, you should set *different completion dates* (maybe 2 or 3 days early) or simply make sure you follow your schedule of hours per day to spend on each assignment. Then all of them should be done on the same day.

- What if you get sick? If you do, try to get lots of rest and get better quickly. If you have scheduled time to have your assignments ready a few days before they are actually due, you can afford to lose a few days.

- What if you prepare your schedule and then discover that you simply have too much work to do in the semester? What if doing all those assignments is impossible or will take more hours per day than you have available? Such questions might just come from fear, when the fact is that you CAN get the assignments done. But it might be a good time to talk to your academic advisor. Sometimes international students take more courses at the same time than is wise. It may be that you will have to drop a course.

Is there a proper way to survive a semester of assignments without needing to ignore your friends and become a person who never leaves your room except to go to the library? Yes, there is. It's a matter of balance.

Though it seems like scheduling your whole semester will make you into a slave, it can actually be the means to make you free. If you know you have 3 hours of work to do on assignments, you can plan your day to give yourself time for other things you enjoy. If you do not schedule yourself, you will have a lot of free time at the beginning of the semester but only hard effort and great stress at the end. It is much better to balance your studies with leisure time right through the semester. But here are some important cautions:

- Stay on schedule. It is no good having a schedule if you break it.

- Get exercise and eat well. If you can avoid people who have colds or the flu, do so. Get a flu shot, even if you have to pay for it. Your health is very important if you are going to succeed with your assignments.

- Never study past 10 p.m. You may laugh at this, but, unless you are a very unusual person, your ability to think clearly is considerably less in the late evening. Those who get into a pattern of studying until 3:00 a.m., then getting up at 11:00 the next morning, tend to miss classes and be much more tired than those who follow a reasonable daily pattern. Robbing yourself of sleep will make you unproductive the next day.

- If you are allowed to have employment for pay, be sure you don't work more than ten hours per week. If you must work more than ten hours, you will likely need to take fewer courses.

- If you do fall behind in your assignments, go to your professors *right away* and explain your problem. While professors do not like to give extensions if you ask for them repeatedly, the occasional request for more time will likely get a good response.

- As you are working on assignments, you may find that you reach a point after a few hours of study when your brain rebels. You can't think of the next sentence to write or you fall asleep over your reading. Rather than simply carrying on with your work, it is better to take a break, even for ten minutes, so that you can refresh yourself to carry on. In fact, taking a couple of short breaks over a three hour study session is good for you. Ten minutes of break during each hour of study will make the work much easier, and you will actually get more done.

- Coffee can help, but having a pattern of drinking it all day will lead to even more tiredness than if you never drank it at all.

Other stimulants like "wake-up pills" or even illegal drugs, give an illusion of helping you be alert, but all of them have serious risks. Stay away from stimulants as much as possible, and follow the path of good food, exercise and lots of sleep.

Assignments are always a challenge, but solid planning and careful work will make sure they get done.

# 5

# *Professors*

It's natural to want to know what your professors will be like. Will they know their subjects well? Will they demand more than you can deliver to them? Can you ask them questions if you don't understand? Will they care about you as a person?

What I have to say will not answer all your questions, because each professor is an individual. Some are helpful and generous with their time. Others may have great knowledge but show less desire to assist their students. Let me tell you what you can reasonably expect from a professor.

## The Training of the Professor

Professors began their lives as ordinary people. Really. They did well in the early years of school and had three characteristics required to reach the levels they have finally gained—intelligence, ability to work hard, and a strong motivation to learn. You will find that your professors are generally enthusiastic about their subjects and seem to have an inner strength that helps them complete very busy schedules.

The average professor has a bachelors degree, a masters degree in some area of specialization and a doctoral degree in an area of study that is even more specialized. Professors have worked extremely hard to reach the position they now have. On average they have spent at least nine years in education beyond high school or secondary school. They know the value of devoting many hours to study and making education a priority. Thus you will find that they usually have little sympathy with students who are lazy or who look for easy ways to avoid doing the hard work of learning.

Professors have a deep love for academic study. They are devoted to the subject area in which they have specialized. In their studies, they have developed both a great deal of knowledge and a number of important skills—critical thinking, research ability, and expert understanding of their field. While you can benefit greatly from their knowledge and skill, you might also find that their years of training have resulted in certain characteristics that make it difficult for them to understand the struggles you are facing:

- They may not be happy when students are uninterested in the subject they are teaching. You need to be realistic that not all subjects will excite you in the same way. But if your professor believes you are bored with his/her subject, you may find that you are not as well accepted in the classroom as students who show enthusiasm. Don't pretend to be excited if you are not, but try to look for something, even in a class you don't find interesting, that captures your attention. The process of learning in the classroom requires cooperation between professor and student. If your professor finds his/her topic exciting, you need to discover something to interest you as well.

- They may have limited understanding of students who struggle with research and writing. Most professors feel totally at home in a library. Most have little problem with starting a research project and writing an essay, or even a book. Professors often do not understand how difficult it is for students who are just learning about Western libraries or methods of writing essays in a Western setting. In some cases you may find that a good reference librarian can help you as much with your writing as your professor can, but you should also use the writing center and ask for help from your professor if you need guidance in your writing. There are professors who really do understand your struggles and are able to help you a great deal.

- Professors usually have a belief that problems can be solved with more training. When you first come to a Western university, you are likely still learning English while you also struggle with a different philosophy of education and new demands for your research and writing. While your professors will try to help you, the one thing you may hear most often is that you need to take more English courses or seminars in writing. Having more training will help you to some extent, but many of your problems in a Western educational setting are not easily solved simply by adding another remedial course to your schedule. One of your biggest needs will be developing your *spoken* English skills. Your professors need to understand that you are in the process of learning a whole new way of education. This may simply require time, not extra courses. Be careful not to assume that taking yet another remedial course will solve all your problems.

## The Personality of the Professor

No two professors are alike. Just like real people, some are helpful, some are less helpful. Some are friendly, some are less friendly. Some like to spend lots of time with their students, others go off to their offices or research as soon as the class is over. In fact, professors are like other people—they come in many varieties.

One reality for most professors is that they live very busy lives. This means that, while they will likely take time for you, they have limited time just for conversation. This does not mean that you should avoid going to your professor if you are having problems in a course you are taking. In general, professors want to know if you are having difficulties. They want to see their students succeed. But be sure you really do need your professor's time before you use it.

## Office Hours

Almost all professors post "office hours," times during the week when they are available to meet in their offices with students. Some will ask you to make an appointment if you want to see them. Others will let you just drop in. If you have a problem with an assignment or you are falling behind or you are troubled by some other issue related to your course, those office hours are your opportunity to get help.

Here are suggestions for visiting your professor:

- Make a decision about whether you really do need to see a professor. If you are struggling with how to write a research paper, you may want to go first to the writing center at your school and get some advice. Not every problem is something your professor needs to solve.

- If you do decide that a visit to the professor is needed, tell him/her your name and the course you are in. Your professor has many students and teaches several courses. Thus you should not expect that a professor will automatically remember your name.

- Bring your syllabus with you if you have any questions related to the course assignments.

- If you are having trouble knowing how to express your question to the professor, write it out in advance and bring the written form with you. Should your professor still have trouble understanding what you are asking, you can show him/her your written question.

- Try to be very clear about what you want. Don't say, "I am having problems with this course." Instead say, "I'm having trouble understanding what to do in assignment #4," or, "I'm falling behind, and I'm not sure I can get assignment #6 done on time."

- Have a possible solution ready if you can think of one. For example, you may want your professor to explain assignment #4 or give you a one week extension for #6. Be plain about what you would like to be done. If your professor has a different solution, you will have to accept it, but it's best to have your own ready first.

- Take written notes of what the professor tells you. If you don't, you will likely forget important details. If you take notes right there in the professor's office, you are saying that his/her advice is important.

I want to take a moment to suggest what might be the worst and best experience you can have if you visit a professor with a problem you are having. The worst is not intended to worry you but to help you prepare to meet a professor who may not be helpful. The best is what I hope you always experience.

Here is absolutely the *worst* situation you might expect when you go to ask you professor for help.

## *Imagine:/*

YOU [at the professor's open office door]: Professor Smith?
PROFESSOR: Yes?
YOU: I wanted to ask you about the research project.
PROFESSOR: Which course?
YOU: Introduction to Ecology. I have the syllabus here.
PROFESSOR [looks at her watch]: What's your problem?
YOU: It says, "Elucidate the arguments of Lynn White and Jackson Ice on the Judeo-Christian responsibility for the environmental crisis." This word, "Elucidate—"
PROFESSOR: Shed light upon. Did you look it up in a dictionary?
YOU: Yes.
PROFESSOR: Then if you have a problem with the assignment, you should go to the writing center. I'm really pretty busy right now.
YOU: I'm sorry. I thought you had office hours now. You said we could come any time during office hours.
PROFESSOR: I can't write your papers for you. If you need help, go to the writing center.
YOU: I've already been there, and they said that I should talk to you.
PROFESSOR: What's the problem exactly with the assignment?

YOU: Elucidate. Do you mean that we should explain the views of White and Ice or we should evaluate their views?

PROFESSOR: You are supposed to elucidate. Shed light on.

YOU: But I don't know what that means in this case—explain or evaluate?

PROFESSOR [pausing for a moment before speaking]: You people should understand that I'm not in this profession to spoon-feed you. It is your responsibility to get your assignments done well and in time. If you can't do that, you shouldn't be here.

YOU: What do you mean when you say, "You people?" My race? My culture? Students like me who don't know Western ways?"

PROFESSOR: I'm sorry. That's not what I meant. Look, I'm very busy. I can't give you extra help without giving it to everybody in the class. Just do your best.

YOU: But I don't understand the assignment.

PROFESSOR: I can't help you. Just read it over again and do your best.

This professor has failed to understand that the assignment itself is ambiguous—it can mean different things depending on how it is interpreted. She has failed to answer your question and has left you in a situation where you might do the assignment wrongly simply because she failed to phrase it correctly. What is more, she seems frustrated and has made a statement that likely shows prejudice against international students.

What can you do?

- Talk to other students in the class to see if they understood the assignment and can agree on what they believe it is asking them to do. But be careful—just because a majority of the class agrees on a certain interpretation does not mean it is correct.

- Ask other students who are uncertain about the meaning of the assignment to go to the professor and try to get a clear interpretation.

- If you believe the professor has made a statement that is prejudiced against international students, you can consider making a complaint to your school's harassment officer (or director of student services). Make such a decision wisely, but you should not have to fear that the professor will give you a bad mark because you complained. Your school will have regulations that prevent retaliation from the professor. If you do follow this route, be sure you write down the date and time of the offence as well as the exact words the professor used. Incidents where a complaint is needed are extremely rare, and you will likely never be in this position. Just be aware that it is possible to make a complaint if you have been made the object of prejudice.

- If you are still uncertain what the professor wants you to do, interpret the assignment as best you can. Attach a note indicating that you believe the assignment was ambiguous, so you chose to do it in this way. Explain your interpretation of the assignment.

That was the worst experience you might have. In fact, I've never known a professor who behaved in this way. This is what you should usually expect to happen.

## *Imagine:*

YOU: [at professor's door] Professor Smith?
PROFESSOR: Yes? Come in.
YOU: I wondered if you could help me understand the research assignment.
PROFESSOR: Intro to Ecology, right?
YOU: Yes, it says we are supposed to elucidate the views of White and Ice.
PROFESSOR: Elucidate. Shed light on.
YOU: Yes, but I don't know what it means for this essay. I went to the writing center, but they didn't know either.
PROFESSOR: What exactly is the problem?

YOU: I don't understand if we are to explain the views of White and Ice or evaluate those views.

PROFESSOR: That would make a big difference, wouldn't it? If you explained their views, you'd just be describing. If you evaluated, you'd be determining what's good and bad about their views. Let me think about this for a second. [She pauses]. I think "elucidate" wasn't the best word to use. Look, change it to "evaluate." I'll tell the other students next class.

YOU: Thank you. That helps a lot.

PROFESSOR: Any other problems?

YOU: No. I think I'll be fine now. Thank you very much.

PROFESSOR: Come back any time you have a question. And thanks for pointing out this problem.

## The Professor's Style of Education

Different professors have a variety of views about good methods of education. Some believe that learning a lot of content is very important. They will tend to lecture and leave the development of your critical thinking skills to you. Others will emphasize critical thinking. Their classes will use a lot of discussion. In most cases, you will easily adapt to your professor's style, but there are some types of professors who may give you some special challenges:

- The Adversarial Professor—This style of educator comes with the belief that students learn best when they are put under a lot of stress. A professor who is adversarial will correct his/her students constantly, almost never praise them for good work and will look for ways to make the course more difficult than it first appears to be. The professor deliberately acts like an adversary (an opponent) of the student in order to motivate the student to do good work.

  The main problem with this style of education is that it doesn't work. Students do not do better with an adversarial professor.

You, as an international student struggling with language and a new approach to education, should not have an adversarial professor, who will make everything harder. If you discover in your first class or two that your professor is adversarial, transfer to another class if you can.

• The Unmotivated Professor—There is one part of the university system that many people know little about. The university is not just a place of teaching. It is a place of research. In smaller colleges, research is not a large part of a professor's life, but in larger universities and particularly in graduate schools, your professors may teach only one or two courses in a semester. The rest of their time is devoted to research.

While it certainly does not happen often, there are some professors who teach only because they have to. It is part of their agreement with the university—they must teach a certain number of classes in order to be permitted to do their research. Such professors may resent the time they have to spend with students and show little motivation to teach well. Fortunately they soon develop a reputation of being poor teachers, so you may be able to avoid them if fellow students warn you soon enough.

• The Careless Professor—Some professors develop a reputation for not covering the course material before the semester ends, taking a very long time to grade assignments, not being on time for classes, or sometimes seeming unprepared to teach. These behaviors could have a number of possible causes:

• The careless professor may simply be very busy. Some professors commit themselves to far too many responsibilities and struggle to keep up with their classes.

• The careless professor may be highly creative but disorganized. The characteristics of being creative but poorly organized often go together. Before you assume you have a bad professor, listen to him/her carefully. Does your professor present new ideas in very interesting ways? Do you find yourself paying attention simply because the professor brings the subject alive for you?

I once had a professor who some might have called "careless." He seemed disorganized and never was on time for anything. But this man could take his subject and make it fascinating. He would often digress (go off the topic), and the class would have no idea where he planned to take us. But eventually he'd return to the subject, and we would discover that the digression had been his way of teaching us something about the subject that we would never have learned otherwise. True, he never covered all the course material before the semester ended, but I learned more from him than from most other professors.

Before you assume that the careless professor will be a problem to you, evaluate what such a professor can provide in a creative approach to the subject you are taking. But beware: some professors are careless simply because they do not like teaching. If that is the case, transfer to another course or another section.

- The Cold Professor—Some professors seem to be unfriendly and distant. This could be a problem if such a professor had no interest in his/her students or their needs. But it may simply be that your professor has a reserved or quiet personality. Before you decide against staying in a class with a cold professor, look for signs that the professor is motivated to teach and shows signs of wanting to be helpful to students. Many "cold" professors are actually excellent teachers.

- The Tough Professor—You may find that other students speak of certain professors as being very "tough." What they mean in that these professors give difficult assignments and expect a lot of good performance from their students. Before you simply avoid a tough professor, ask yourself whether you really want to learn the subject that professor is teaching. Sometimes a tough professor may be just the person to teach you more than you might learn in another class. But be careful. Make sure you can do the tough professor's assignments and still be able to complete the assignments in your other classes on time. Never take two courses from tough professors in one semester.

How can you be sure that a professor will be good or bad for you? You should first know that most professors are highly skilled people who really care about their students and want to provide a first-class education. Problem professors are few, and their reputations are generally known. A good source of guidance is other students who may be a year or two ahead of you. They will be happy to tell you their good experiences and bad experiences. But be careful: one student may have had problems with a certain professor, while others did not. You need to listen to the advice of several students.

Despite the warnings I've presented, I want you to be able to enroll in courses with confidence that your professor is going to be a real benefit to you. I believe you will be amazed both by the knowledge of your professors and by their ability to teach you well. Professors are wonderful people who work very hard, use excellent methods and show strong enthusiasm for their subjects.

## The Mentoring Relationship

International students tend to honor their professors highly. In the discipleship model of education that they knew in their homelands, the professor acted as a mentor, a guide for life rather than simply a teacher of knowledge. The better students could expect that their professors would notice them and want to spend more time with them.

In North America, however, professors generally do not see themselves as mentors who will have a large impact on their students' lives. Professors are there to teach courses. While they are teaching, their students are important to them. But when the course is over, the professor moves on to a new group of students, and the relationship with students in his/her previous course generally ends. There are exceptions. One of my students from Korea, who I first met many years ago, has now graduated, and we remain good friends. But that is truly an exception. While I am happy to be with the students I teach, I simply do not have the time to mentor them in an ongoing way, that is to spend extra hours teaching them additional things or helping them to grow as persons. I try to help students when I can, but I do not develop strong relationships with every one of them.

Some international students may believe that, because a professor gave them some special help, that professor wants to have a special relationship with them as a guide or mentor. These students are often disappointed when the relationship does not continue or when the professor, a semester later, has forgotten their name. This is not a deliberate insult. It is simply that professors in the West teach students *within courses*. When the course is over, the teacher-student relationship is complete as well. The professor may greet you next semester and be friendly to you, but you no longer are his/her student in any official way.

When a professor does give you extra help, you may believe that the professor will also be kinder to you when grades are assigned than s/he is to other students. I have had international students say to me, "You will be good to me when you grade my assignment?" What they are asking me to do is give them a better mark because we have had a relationship in which I have helped them. But in a Western setting, I cannot do that. I am required to treat all students in the same way. I cannot have favorite students.

International students, who have learned to honor their professors, are often disappointed in the West when their professors see the teacher-student relationship as something that is short term. In your home country, your professor was a mentor, a guide, someone who would continue to be involved in your growth as a student. In the West, your relationship with your professor will not usually be a mentoring one. You will learn from him/her within your course, but the relationship will not usually last beyond the end of the semester. It is not that your professors do not like you—they do. But the Western model of education is different.

You should not expect that your professor will want to develop a social relationship with you outside of class. This will be unlikely, not because the professor refuses to be your friend, but because professors cannot show favoritism to one student. Take note, as well, that students in the West usually do not give their professors gifts.

Your relationships with your professors can be friendly and happy ones. But the West does not have a discipleship model to any great extent. Thus the professor-student relationship remains strong only while you are taking your course.

# 6

# *The Library*

## The Purpose of an Academic Library

Many students think of a library as a just collection of books and journals. As an international student walking into a Western university library, you may never have seen so many books and journals in one place before. Your first questions may be: "Where do I begin? How can I possibly find what I need?"

Rather than thinking of the library as a *collection* of printed materials, it is better to think of the library as a *source of information.* That information may be found in books or journals or videos or electronic databases. The important thing to remember is that you are looking for *information.*

In the library, there are ways to locate that information more easily. If you understand these ways, using a library will not be as difficult as you thought it would be.

## The Parts of an Academic Library

Before we look at methods to find the information you need, it is important to understand where you are going. Let us take a tour of an average academic library:

- **Circulation Counter**—As you enter a library, you will probably see a counter with people behind it. This is the place where you will sign out the books you want to take with you. More about this counter and how to sign out books will be found below.

- **The Catalog**—The catalog is usually near the entrance of the library as well, although, because it is usually electronic, you may find stations of it in several places in the library. What is a catalog? It is an index of names, titles and subjects related to the book collection in the library you are using. Think of it as a guide to help you locate books that you need. These days, almost all catalogs are in computer format. We will look at the use of a library catalog in a short while.

- **The Reference Collection**—As you move further into the library, you will find an area labeled "Reference Books" or "Reference Collection." These are books that are to be consulted within the library only. In most cases you cannot sign them out and take them home.

What are reference books? They are dictionaries, encyclopedias, handbooks, manuals, atlases, and so on. Each has been produced to allow the user to look up brief information. You are probably familiar with word dictionaries that allow you to look up definitions or translate from one language to another. But there are also dictionaries and encyclopedias on almost any subject you could imagine—religion, psychology, sociology, history, and even baseball.

These reference books are concerned with more than just the meanings of words. They explain the major concepts and people involved with particular subjects. For example, in a dictionary or encyclopedia of psychology, you might look up "behaviorism" or "personality theories" or "Freud, Sigmund," and find a paragraph or even several pages that explain each subject. In a dictionary of theology, you might find "atonement" or "Calvinism" or "Thomas Aquinas," and some brief information that explains each of these.

The advantage of reference books is that they give you enough basic information about a topic to help you search intelligently for more information. As well, an article in a reference book will often explain the important controversies and questions involved in that topic.

Your library may also have reference works available on CD-ROM or through the Internet. These formats offer a lot of advantages in the ability to search for information that would normally appear under several different headings in a print reference work.

- **The Circulating Collection**—This is usually the largest part of the library collection. It consists of books that can be signed out and taken home. If you are used to a small library, you probably found books by walking through the library and looking at the shelves until you saw what you wanted. *This is not a useful method in a larger academic library. There are too many books, and you will only waste your time.* If you want to find the books you need easily, you will have to use the catalog. More information on use of the catalog will be provided below.

- **The Periodical Collection**—Periodicals are magazines and journals that are delivered to the library at regular intervals—daily, weekly, monthly, quarterly or annually. You've already experienced periodicals, even if you've only read a newspaper or *Time Magazine.*

These days, the trend is toward providing periodicals in electronic form. Electronic full text periodicals have been available for several years now, and students have a great hunger for this format. Academic libraries are buying more and more periodicals electronically, often within periodical indexes. We will discuss this in greater detail when we look at periodical indexes, below.

With periodicals that come in print form, libraries bind them, resulting in many years of a magazine or journal bound in several volumes. These volumes are usually arranged in a periodicals area by the title of the periodical.

Many libraries have older years of periodicals only in microfiche or microfilm forms. You will need to use a microfiche or microfilm reader to read them. There are usually reader-printers to copy microfiche or microfilm onto printers. A microfiche looks like a photographic negative except that it is on a sheet that is about 4" X 6" in size. If you hold a microfiche up to the light, you will see that it is pages of information printed very small, too small to read unless you use a microfiche reader, which is a machine that projects the microfiche image in magnified form on a screen. Microfilm is in a roll rather than a flat sheet, and needs its own special machine in order for you to read it. *If you have difficulty using microfiche or microfilm, ask a librarian for assistance.*

An academic library will usually have a catalog to the periodicals that it collects, listing which periodicals the library has and what years and volumes are available. The catalog will tell you if the periodical comes in electronic, paper, microfiche or microfilm. Where will you find such a catalog? Many libraries have it in computerized form. Others use a printout in a binder or a card file to indicate which periodicals it has. *If you cannot locate the periodical catalog, ask a reference librarian.*

Here are some things you should know about periodicals:

- Most periodical publishers assign a volume number to their periodical for each year it is published. Thus the first year of a periodical will be volume 1, the second year volume 2, and so on. Each issue of a periodical is also numbered. Thus you will have volume 1, issue 1; volume 1, issue 2; volume 1, issue 3; and so on.

- Some periodicals begin each new issue with page 1. Others continue the numbering right through all the issues of the year. Thus issue 1 might end on page 117. Issue 2 will begin on page 118. If issue 2 ends on page 236, issue 3 will begin on page 237. The reason periodicals do this is that they expect the library to bind the whole year's issues at the end of the year. When it is bound, the volume will be numbered in order, from page 1 to page 436.

- There is no library that has all the periodical titles that are published. In every library, you will find only *some* of all the periodicals available in the world.

- **Periodical Indexes**—How does a person find periodical articles on a particular topic? One method might be to locate many issues of a particular periodical and look through tables of contents, hoping that one of them will have an article that is suitable for the topic. But that method could take a very long time.

  The other way is to consult a periodical index. Periodical indexes do for periodical articles what the book catalog does for the library—they provide a means for you to search for articles by subject or keyword no matter what journal or magazine contains these articles. There are general periodical indexes which deal with many topics, and also indexes which are specially designed for various subject disciplines: Psychology, Sociology, Literature, History, Religion, and so on.

  Most indexes, these days, are in computerized form, though, because they often provide indexing only to journals from the late 1980s to the present, libraries usually have print indexes for earlier years. With a computerized index, you can enter subject words or key words, and you will be provided with a list of articles from many journals. NOTE: *It is very important to record at least of the title of the Journal (e.g.* Journal of the American Scientific Affiliation), *the journal volume, and the page numbers in order to identify that article in a bibliography.*

Many periodical indexes offer you the *full electronic text* of the articles you locate. This means that the index not only gives you a list of articles on your topic from various journals but provides the full text of the article right on the screen. Full text generally comes in two forms: HTML (sometimes just a simple text file, sometimes in XML format) and PDF. With PDF, you have to click on an icon to get the text of the article, and your computer will have to have Adobe Acrobat loaded (you can obtain it for free from the Internet). PDF files look like photocopies of the original printed pages of the journal and generally take longer to load than do HTML files. With HTML files, you get quick loading, but you usually lose the original look and page numbers of the print edition.

If you are using an index in your institution's library, you can print the articles or send them to your e-mail address. But most universities now offer you off-campus connection to indexes, so you can search the indexes from your own computer, even if you live miles away from the campus.

Every periodical index has its own features and searching abilities. The best way to get to know them is to use them a lot and try various kinds of searches. Remember that some indexes are better for some topics than others. It's useless to search for articles on English literature in an index devoted to medicine.

While electronic full text is very popular with students, not all journals are yet available in this format. You will still need to locate some articles in paper or microfiche or microfilm. If you have an article citation (the basic information about an article) and it is not in full text, the library may still have it. Check the library's own periodical catalog (often a computerized list or found right in the library's book catalog) to see if it's available in some other format.

- **Other Materials**—Your library will probably have CDs, audio cassettes, DVDs and video cassettes available, as well as government documents and various special collections. Ask the reference librarian to tell you what materials of these types are available. There are specialized indexes available for some of them, but you will likely need to consult a librarian to learn how to best locate such resources.

## Using the Library Catalog

Most library catalogs are now in computer format. Here are some of the basic facts that you need to know:

- **The Catalog Record**—Here is a sample catalog record such as you might find in a computerized library catalog:

| | |
|---|---|
| **Call Number** | Z710 .B21 2000 |
| **Title** | Research strategies: Finding your way through the information fog |
| **Author** | Badke, William B., 1949- |
| **Publisher** | San Jose: Writers Club Press, 2000. |
| **Description** | x, 181 p.: ill.; 24 cm. |
| **ISBN** | 0595100821 |
| **Subject(s)** | Research—Methodology—Handbooks, manuals, etc. Information retrieval. Online bibliographic searching. Report writing—Handbooks, manuals, etc. |
| **Gen. Note(s)** | "This book is a substantial revision of The survivor's guide to library research (Grand Rapids: Zondervan Publishing House, 1990)." |

What you have in a catalog record is all the information you need to locate the book. The *call number* is especially important. This will be the number on the spine of the book when you find it on the shelf. (More information on call numbers is provided below.)

- **Searching for Books in a Library Catalog**—The important thing to remember is that, with a computer catalog, you can usually search for anything that is in a catalog record. Thus, if you want to find a book by someone named "Badke," you can type in his name as an "author" search. If you know the book you are looking for is *Research Strategies,* you can type that title as a title search. If you are looking for books on library research, you could type "library research" as a keyword search. In each case, the catalog would give you the catalog record above.

There are many different kinds of computer catalog. Each of them will look different on the screen, but each of them does the same thing—provide you with an index so that you can search for the book you want and get a call number from the catalog record so that you can find the book on the library shelf. When you come to a type of catalog which you haven't seen before, *it is very important to read the instructions on the screen or to find a nearby instruction manual or to ask a reference librarian for help.* Don't spend hours becoming worried because you can't understand how to use the computer. Look for written guidelines or for a reference librarian to help you.

If you want instruction on how to do computer searches well, locate a copy of the book described in the catalog record above: *Research Strategies: Finding your Way through the Information Fog,* produced by iUniverse.com/Writer's Club Press.

# Classification Systems

There are two classification systems most commonly in use in North America—*Dewey Decimal Classification* and *The Library of Congress Classification System.* Before we look at each, let us see what a classification system does.

We saw that the catalog can tell you if a book by a certain author or with a certain title is in the library. You can also search for subject headings or keywords to get a list of the library's books on a certain topic. But how do you actually locate those books in the library? If a library has only 200 volumes, this is not too much of a problem. You simply look through the 200 books until you find the ones you want. To help you, the library could arrange all its books on the shelves alphabetically by author. Or it could assign a number to each book as it came into the collection. Then if you wanted *Research Strategies,* you could note from the catalog record that it is book number 186, and you could just go along the shelves until you got to the 186th book. It would have a 186 on its spine.

But there is a reason why libraries are not organized by the author's name or by book numbers—Students like to see books on the same topic *grouped together.* For example, all the books about Sigmund Freud should be on the same shelf.

Small libraries could arrange their books by broad subjects—the sociology books here and the psychology books over there. But as libraries grow bigger, it becomes more difficult to find what you want. Classification systems have been developed *to help a library to group similar books together* so that students can see several books on their topic all in the same place.

Both of the classification systems we will be discussing below began in the same way: They divided up all of knowledge into a number of headings and assigned letters and/or numbers to each heading.

Let's look at each one:

- **The Library of Congress Classification System**—This system begins with one or two letters of the alphabet, followed by numbers. An example would be BL625. The alphabet letter(s) tell you what the broad subject is, as follows:

| | |
|---|---|
| **A** | General Works |
| **B-BJ** | Philosophy, Psychology |
| **BL-BX** | Religion |
| **C** | Auxiliary Sciences of History |
| **D** | History: General and Old World (Eastern Hemisphere) |
| **E-F** | History: America (Western Hemisphere) |
| **G** | Geography, Anthropology, Recreation |
| **H** | Social Sciences |
| **J** | Political Science |
| **KD** | Law of the United Kingdom and Ireland |
| **KF** | Law of the United States |
| **L** | Education |
| **M** | Music |
| **N** | Fine arts |
| **P-PA** | General philology and linguistics Classical languages and literature |
| **PB-PH** | Modern European languages |
| **PJ-PM** | Languages and literatures of Asia, Africa, Oceania, American Indian languages, artificial languages |

(There are further language subdivisions for **PN-PT**, which are not listed here

| | |
|---|---|
| **Q** | Science |
| **R** | Medicine |

| S | Agriculture |
|---|---|
| T | Technology |
| U | Military Science |
| V | Naval Science |
| Z | Bibliography, Library science |

To find a book with the classification number BL625, you must go to the part of the library where the B's begin, then move along the shelves until you reach the BL's (the signs at the end of each row should help you to find the area you want). Then move along the BL's until you find BL625.

You will notice on the catalog record that you do not just have a classification number to look up (such as BL625), but other things as well, for example BL625 .W42 1998. If you were to see that whole number on the spine of a book, it might be printed as:

```
BL
625
.W42
1999
```

While BL625 was a classification number, BL625 .W42 1998 is referred to as a *call number.* In a larger library, the call number gives additional information so that you can locate the right book. If you go to the section of the library that has books with BL625 on their spines, you will find that there are several such books. The library needs to arrange these in some kind of order. What most libraries have chosen is a *cutter* system, a letter and number system that is alphabetical and is usually based on the author's last name. Thus, when you get to the BL625's, you need to look at the next line, lower on the spine. By reading the letters in alphabetical order, you can locate .W42.

Here is how it works. Imagine that you have come to the BL625 section of the library, and there are several books with the same BL625. They will be arranged in alphabetical order as follows—notice how the *cutter* tells you the order, first by the letter used, and then by the number:

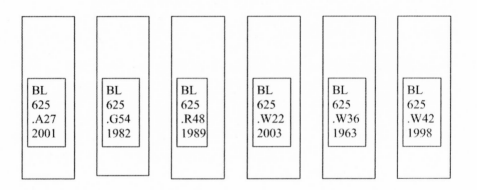

The date is generally not very important, except when you have two editions of the same book.

- **Dewey Decimal Classification**—Dewey Decimal Classification uses only numbers for its classification plan. It divides all knowledge like this:

| | |
|---|---|
| **000** | Generalities |
| **100** | Philosophy and related disciplines |
| **200** | Religion |
| **300** | Social sciences |
| **400** | Language |
| **500** | Pure sciences |

| 600 | Technology (Applied sciences) |
|-----|-------------------------------|
| 700 | The arts Fine and decorative arts |
| 800 | Literature |
| 900 | General geography and history and their auxiliaries |

Within each of the 100 numbers, the Dewey system subdivides knowledge in that discipline even further. For example, part of the **900** (geography and history) section includes these numbers:

| 900 | General geography and history |
|-----|-------------------------------|
| 910 | General geography Travel |
| 913 | Geography of the ancient world |
| 930 | General history of the ancient world |
| 940 | General history of Europe |
| 950 | General history of Asia |
| 951 | China & adjacent areas |
| 952 | Japan & adjacent islands |
| 954 | South Asia India |

and so on.

Because there is so much knowledge in the world, further subdivisions were needed. Thus, Dewey added decimal points and then more numbers, sometimes a lot of them. The culture of ancient Egypt, for example, is 913.32, and the Habsburg rulers of Austria are 943.604.

It is easy to find most books with Dewey Decimal numbers, as long as you remember the following:

- You must begin with the first three numbers of the classification number and locate that place on the shelves. If there is a decimal point and more numbers, then move along the shelves to your *right* until you find the right classification.

- A classification number in Dewey may be so long that it continues on the next line. Thus 227.1077 may look like this on the spine of the book:

227.1
077

- Dewey Decimal Classification uses the same *cutter* method that Library of Congress uses (see section A. above). Thus you will find that the catalog will show a number like this: 226.067 .H272 1997, which on the spine of the book will look like this:

226.067
.H272
1997

- Dewey Decimal numbers are *decimal.* Thus they run in this order:
306.7
306.72
306.724
306.8
306.85
306.9

# Signing Out Books

When you want to borrow books to take with you, you need to know the rules for taking out books. Each library has its own set of rules, and so you must obtain and read the regulations provided by that library. The rules will usually be posted on the library's Internet page.

Here are some procedures and suggestions:

- In most libraries, certain books can be signed out (borrowed) and certain books cannot. Usually reference books cannot be signed out. In many libraries, periodicals cannot be signed out. If you are in doubt, read the library regulations or ask someone at the circulation desk.

- If you want to borrow books, you will need to find them yourself and bring them to the circulation desk. Library staff will not do this for you. Normally, you will have to show a borrower's card *for that library* in order to borrow books. If you are using a library for which you do not have a card, you may need to pay money to obtain one, though many universities have agreements among themselves to allow free borrowing at one another's libraries.

- When you sign out a book, you may have to sign your name on a card, or your name may be entered automatically into a computer. In some cases, students sign out books themselves. If you do not know how to sign out a book, just tell the staff member that you have not signed out books there before. The staff member will tell you what to do.

- Many colleges and universities also have a selection of *reserve* materials that are normally held at the circulation desk. These are materials that a professor wants all of his or her students to use. Such books or articles have a short borrowing period, which may be as long as three days or as short as two hours. Usually the professor will tell the student which books have been placed on reserve. You may then ask at the circulation desk for the books you need, and borrow them for the length of time indicated.

- Be sure to notice when your books are to be returned. Record that date on your calendar so that you will remember when to return your books. If you are done with your books earlier than this date, you should return them early so that others may use them. Often you can renew your books (sign them out again) one or two times. If you return your books late, however, you will have to pay a fine. Returning books late is unkind to other students who may have been waiting to use those books.

## Some Final Advice

- If you are not familiar with the library you are using, take this manual with you and **_explore_** the library. Locate all the parts of it—circulation desk, catalog, reference collection, and so on. Spend an hour getting to know the library as well as you can.

- Never be afraid to ask library staff for help. It is their job is to help students, and they are very good at answering questions. If you are seeking help with an assignment, bring your syllabus with you. If you are not sure the librarian will understand what you are looking for, write out your question on a piece of paper and show it to the librarian. (More about librarians will be found in Chapter Ten: "Important People to Know in Your Academic World.")

- Do not let a fear of libraries stop you from enjoying them. Most students feel nervous in a library at first. The more time you spend in the library, the easier it will be to use.

# 7

## *Writing Research Papers*

The research essay is a common assignment in North American higher education. The concept of the research essay at first appears simple:

- Choose a topic
- Do research on the topic
- Write an essay based on your research

But it is really not simple at all. International students often are very disappointed when they receive their first essay back from a professor. The comments may include:

- "No research question"
- "Too general" or "Not sufficiently narrow"
- "Improper use of sources"
- "Much of this material appears to be plagiarized"
- "Inadequate bibliography"
- "No periodical literature"

and so on.

This chapter will show you what North American professors expect from students doing research essays. Let's begin with the topic:

## Topic Selection and Analysis

It is obvious that a research essay must have a topic, but what sort of topic? Some professors will give you a list and ask you to choose one. Others will provide you with general guidelines only. For example, you might be taking a course on "The History of the Middle Ages in Europe" and be told to write a paper on some important person of that period, showing how his/her life influenced the Middle Ages.

The first thing you will need to assume is that your topic is likely to be too broad, that is, it will require you to deal with too much information for one essay. If you leave the topic broad, it will be superficial. Picture it like this: You have two lakes, one small but deep, the other large but shallow.

The wide but shallow lake is like a broad topic. You can say many things about the topic, but everything you say will be at a very basic or survey level. For example, if you were writing an essay on the development of industrialization in Korea, you could say many things, but you could not, for example, go into in depth analysis about the effect that the Asian financial crisis of the late 1990's had on the progress of automobile manufacturing in Korea.

The narrow lake is like taking your broad topic and choosing to deal with only one part of it, but now in depth. For example, instead of writing a history of the development of industrialization in Korea, you could choose only one time period along with one industry and narrow your topic to "The effect of the Asian financial crisis of the late 1990's on automobile manufacturing in Korea." Now you have room to do more analysis and get deeper into the subject.

> **In the North American academic setting, professors usually want you to narrow your topic to allow for depth. You do this by choosing to deal with only one part of the topic, not all of it.**

## The Research Question

Many students believe that the purpose of a research essay is to **report** on the books and articles they have read. They think the professor wants them simply to quote from or summarize what they've read so that the result is an essay that tells the reader all about the topic. *This, however, is not the purpose of a research essay.*

> **A research essay is intended to allow you to answer a question or controversy related to the topic you are studying.**

**How can a student develop a proper research question?**

- Narrow your topic as described in **Topic Selection and Analysis** above.

- Use reference sources or short introductions to your topic in books to discover aspects of the topic that are controversial or need investigation.

- Develop a few possible research questions based on what you find in reference sources. These should be one sentence questions that are simple and clear.

- Choose **one** of these questions to be the research question for your essay.

Take note that every research essay should have only one research question. You do not want to have an essay that states, "The following paper will examine _____ and will also _____ and will also _____." You want to deal with only one question in any research project.

**Here are some examples:**

- You start with a topic like: **"The history of industrial development in Korea."** You choose one aspect and narrow your topic to **"The history of the automobile industry in Korea during the Asian Financial Crisis of the late 1990s."** Then you develop a research question: **"What was the influence of the Asian Financial Crisis of the late 1990s on the automobile industry in Korea?"**

- You start with the topic, **"Constantine"** (Roman emperor of the 300s AD who declared his approval of Christianity, leading to it becoming the official religion of the Roman Empire under Theodosius, 379-395). You narrow down to: **"The Conversion of Constantine."** From your basic reading you discover that there is a controversy—some people believe that Constantine did not really have a conversion to Christianity but pretended to do so because he knew it was politically better to endorse Christianity than to persecute Christians. Thus you create a research question: **"Was the conversion of Constantine real?"**

- You start with the topic, **"Euthanasia"** (that is, helping very ill people to end their lives). As you begin research, you discover that euthanasia is legal under certain conditions in the Netherlands. So you narrow to **"Euthanasia in the Netherlands."** Also, from your reading you discover the argument of some people that once euthanasia is legalized, this will lead to the death of people who did not want to die (very elderly people, the disabled, etc.) This is called a "slippery slope argument," which says that once your feet slip on a hillside, you will slide all the way to the bottom of the hill. Similarly, the argument is that once you allow certain people to kill other people, the killing will increase until many people who didn't want to die are also killed. Thus your research question could be: **"Is there evidence from the Netherlands euthanasia experience that legalizing euthanasia creates a slippery slope?"** Your research would investigate what is being done with euthanasia now that it is legal in the Netherlands.

For more information in narrowing topics and creating research questions, see Chapter One of William Badke, *Research Strategies: Finding your Way through the Information Fog.* San Jose: Writers Club Press, 2000.

# Structure of a Research Paper

The way you structure or outline your research paper is very important. It must have definite sections to it:

- **Introduction**—The introduction serves two purposes. First, it allows you to provide the reader with some brief background information about the topic. Second, it lets you state your research question. Note that your research question must *always* be in your introduction.

- **The Body**—The body of the research essay is the main part. It is generally broken down into various headings that deal with aspects of your topic. **It is not easy to decide what headings should be in the body or in what order they should come.** You must look at your topic and ask yourself, "What issues must I cover in order to answer my research question?" This may mean that you need a section to describe the controversy in depth, a section to answer the arguments of someone who does not agree with your position, and a section to make a strong case for your position being true. Here are some examples from the topics we discussed in **The Research Question** above:

**"What was the influence on the automobile industry in Korea of the Asian Financial Crisis of the late 1990s?"**

I. Introduction
II. Initial Effect on the Automobile Industry
III. Later Effect on the Automobile Industry
IV. Was the Effect Positive or Negative?
V. Conclusion

**"Was the religious conversion of Constantine real?"**

I. Introduction
II. Arguments that the conversion was real
III. Arguments that the conversion was not real
IV. Conclusion

**"Is there evidence from the Netherlands euthanasia experience that legalizing euthanasia creates a slippery slope?"**

I. Introduction
II. The Laws that Control Euthanasia in the Netherlands
III. Actual use of Euthanasia Laws in the Netherlands
IV. Is there evidence that Doctors are going beyond the Controls of the Euthanasia Laws?
V. Conclusion

- **The Conclusion**—The conclusion summarizes your research and answers your research question.

For more on structure, outline, etc. see William Badke, *Research Strategies,* Chapter Ten.

# What is Proper Research Essay Form?

International students soon discover that professors want research papers to be presented in certain ways. The professor may say, "This is what your title page should look like." Or he/she may indicate that you need to follow "APA Format." The issue of what an essay is supposed to look like can be quite a problem.

## Style Manuals

There are several books available that explain proper form for research papers. They cover everything from what a title page should look like to proper form for notes and bibliography. Three major formats are used in North American universities: APA format, MLA format and Turabian format. Different institutions use different formats. Sometimes even different professors in the same institution will use different formats. Each format has its own book to describe it. These are:

**American Psychological Association. *Publication Manual of the American Psychological Association*. Washington, DC: American Psychological Association.**

**Gibaldi, Joseph. *MLA Handbook for Writers of Research Papers*. New York Modern Language Association.**

**Turabian, Kate L. *A Manual for Writers of Term Papers, Theses, and Dissertations*. Chicago: University of Chicago Press.**

For shorter explanations of the proper forms for notes (footnotes, endnotes, short notes), there are lots of Internet sites that can provide guidance. Note that these Internet addresses can change or disappear, so I cannot guarantee they will be available when you want to locate them. If you need to find other sites, use the search engine google.com, and search for "APA format" or "Turabian format" or "MLA format." Here are some good sites:

## APA

**http://www.wooster.edu/psychology/apa-crib.html**
**http://webster.commnet.edu/apa/apa_index.htm**
**http://cal.bemidji.msus.edu/WRC/Handouts/APAFormat.html**

## MLA

**http://www.hcc.hawaii.edu/education/hcc/library/mlahcc.html**
**http://owl.english.purdue.edu/handouts/research/r_mla.html**
**http://www.english.uiuc.**
**edu/cws/wworkshop/MLA/bibliographymla.htm**

### Turabian (also called Chicago)

**http://www.libs.uga.edu/ref/turabian.html**—Note with Turabian that both a footnote/endnote and a short note format are given. Ask your professor which is the preferred format for your school)
**http://faculty.ucc.edu/egh-damerow/bibliographies.htm**
**http://www.bridgew.edu/depts/maxwell/turabian.htm**

### Several Formats plus Sample Essays in Each Format

**http://www.dianahacker.com/resdoc/**

### For Electronic Items in your Bibliography—all 3 Formats Above:

**http://owl.english.purdue.edu/handouts/research/**
**r_docelectric.html**

There are now electronic formatting tools available electronically that can help you to make sure your papers are in proper format. Check out these Internet sites for information:

APA: **http://www.apastyle.org/** (Look for link to APA Style Helper)
MLA: **http://www.noodletools.com/**
Turabian: **http://www.styleease.com/** (Also has a program for APA)

For a website that collects information on various kinds of software to help write papers and format bibliographies, see: **http://www.wabashcenter.wabash.edu/Internet/software.htm**.

If you are confused about format, your institution may have some sample essays that show you what a title page should look like; how to format your margins, headings and notes; how to set up your bibliography, and so on. See also **http://www.dianahacker.com/resdoc/**. In most academic settings in North America, proper format is important. Take it seriously.

> **The rule with format is to find out what format your professor or school is using, then study it closely and follow it very carefully. Even the punctuation is important. Make sure your notes and bibliography are in exactly the form your professor requires. If you are having any difficulty understanding the form, go to your professor and ask for more help.**

## In Conclusion

The goal of the North American research essay is *not* to gather information and report on it. Research essays are assigned so that you can study a certain topic, develop a research question, and answer it using the materials you have studied *plus* your own analysis. The professor wants to see that you are thinking through an issue, not simply explaining or quoting what you have read. The information you discover in your research is thus only the foundation, the first part, of the task. What is more important is your ability to *use* that information to advance our knowledge.

# EXCURSUS—What's the Big Problem with Plagiarism?

I recently received an e-mail from a colleague in Hong Kong. He was unhappy that I'd written a website for International students on research papers and included a section on plagiarism. He wondered why it was always the international students who were accused of plagiarism, as if Western students never plagiarized, only students from other countries. My answer to him was that Western students also plagiarize, but international students, because of their struggles with English, are more likely to be caught. I had written the website on plagiarism, as I write this excursus, not to accuse international students, but to warn them so that they will never have a problem with this issue.

## What is Plagiarism?

Plagiarism can be defined as *using another writer's words or unique ideas as if they were your own.* It happens when you put those words or ideas into your research paper without indicating that they did not come from you. The professor believes those are your own words or ideas, because you have not stated that they came from someone else.

As such, plagiarism is fraud and is generally punished severely, from getting a zero on your assignment, to failing the course, to being expelled from the university, depending on the regulations of the institution you are in.

It can take several forms:

- The most serious type of plagiarism is simply quoting from a source (a book or article) but not giving any indication by quotation marks and a note that it actually is a quotation from

97

someone else. On very rare occasion a student will actually submit a whole essay written by someone else. Even if this is not the case, you are plagiarizing every time you quote from someone else without indicating that it is a quotation. Some students have tried to avoid accusation by quoting large portions from sources, not using quotation marks but adding notes (footnotes or endnotes or short notes) at the end of each paragraph. This, however, is still plagiarism. So is copying from sources without quotation marks, then listing those sources in your bibliography. Unless you put quotation marks around your quotations and add bibliographical notes, you are giving the reader the impression that the material is your own work.

- It is also possible to plagiarize by using a writer's unique ideas without indicating the source of those ideas. What is a "unique idea?" It is an idea that you find only in one author, not several. It is an idea that **belongs** to that author. If you refer to the idea in your essay without indicating who first expressed that idea, you are leaving the false impression that the idea is your own.

## Why is plagiarism so serious a problem?

The main reason why academic institutions punish plagiarism so strictly is that it is *academic dishonesty*, the telling of a lie. When you use another person's words or ideas in your paper without indicating their source, you are giving the impression that those are *your* words or ideas, when they are not. Remember that professors in North America are more interested in your *interpretation* of your sources than they are in quotations. If you mislead a professor by pretending that what is in your essay came from you, it will result in serious penalties when you are discovered.

# How would a professor find out that I plagiarized material?

It is relatively easy for professors to detect plagiarism from International students. In your home country the use of quotations from great scholars may even have been encouraged. If an your written English is not strong, there is a temptation simply to quote from scholars who have better English. Your professor, however, can easily see the difference between the scholarly English of a plagiarized essay and the less polished English you may use in class or on an examination. Thus, for an international student, excellent English in an essay can be a sign to the professor that the essay might be plagiarized.

These days, professors can find almost any material plagiarized from the Internet or an electronic full text database. Some institutions use plagiarism detection services like turnitin.com. Even if your institution does not, your professor can take a few words of text from your paper, type them, with quotation marks around them, into google.com and locate the exact website from which you plagiarized your material, if indeed, you did. The same can be done with searches in electronic databases provided by companies like ProQuest, EBSCO, Gale, and so on.

In the case of print materials that may have been plagiarized, professors will often go to a library and try to locate the original sources that they believe were copied. If they find these sources, the plagiarism can be proven.

Most international students are honest and have no intention of deceiving a professor. Once you understand that all quotations and use of unique ideas must be clearly indicated in your essay by quotation marks and/or notes, the risk that you will plagiarize will be very small.

For an Internet site designed for professors but providing a lot of information about how to avoid plagiarism, see **http://www. virtualsalt.com/antiplag.htm.**

# How to Avoid Plagiarism

- **Should you use the words of others or your own words?**

Many international students are confused by research assignments in the North American setting. They have been trained to read the work of scholars in books and journals and to present that work in the research essay. Often that has involved quoting many scholars directly so that the research essay is primarily the quotations of other people. There seems to be good reason to do this: We honor great scholars by quoting them, and often their use of language is far better than our own.

---

**But in the North American setting, most research essays are to be presented mostly *in your own words*.**

---

This is confusing. The professor does want you to read the books and articles of other people. The research essay is supposed to make use of that research to present your own analysis and arguments. *But how can a student use the work of others if he/she is not allowed to quote their work?* Here is the answer: You ***are*** allowed to quote from the things you have read, but there are definite rules for doing this:

- The quotations should be short (usually 5 lines or less) and few. My own suggestion is to have no more than one short quotation per page of your essay. One every two or three pages is not too few.

- All quotations must have quotation marks (" ") around them to make it clear that they are quotations.

- All quotations must have a note (footnote, endnote, or short note) attached to them so that it's very clear what source you are quoting. Every item quoted must also be in your bibliography. In the North American setting, you cannot just quote long paragraphs without using quotation marks then put a note after them indicating what source you used. Your quotations must follow the rules above.

- Most of your work is to be in your own words.

This means:

- That you show you have understood what you are reading by interpreting it in your own words.

- That you are not just paraphrasing. Paraphrasing involves rewriting each sentence of something you have read, changing the wording a little bit. *This is not enough to make the material "your own words."*

- That you show that you can interpret what the writer is saying without needing to use many of the writer's words. Let me use an example:

---

**Your friend says to you, "I haven't eaten for a long time, so why don't we stop at McDonalds?" Someone nearby says, "What does he want?" You explain, "My friend is hungry and wants to stop for a burger."**

---

Notice that you did not paraphrase, as for example, "My friend hasn't eaten for a long time and wants to stop at McDonalds." You actually interpreted what your friend said and expressed it accurately but in your own words. The only word from your friend that you also used was "stop."

Here's an excerpt from an article that I published on the Internet on the significance of electronic documents. The original paragraph is:

Thus an electronic document disrupts the very meaning of the word "document." Electronically, a "document" can be viewed from anywhere in the world at the same time via the Internet, can have its wording and its look changed at will without any sign left behind that there was an earlier version, and can encompass other documents as well as encourage reading out of order. This may seem exciting (for example, we can hyperlink a document so that any possible problem or interest a reader may experience can be answered with the click of a mouse) but it carries dangers as well. ("Electronic Documents are Different," http://www.acts.twu.ca/lbr/electronicdocs.htm).

A paraphrase, which would *not* be acceptable, might read:

Therefore an electronic document upsets the actual meaning of the word "document." In electronic form, a "document" can be seen all over the world all at once via the Internet, can have its words and what it looks like altered at will without having left behind any indication that there was an earlier form, and can include other documents as well as support the idea of reading out of order. This might seem good, but it carries dangers as well.

Notice that I've borrowed sentence structure and even words from the original without really interpreting it. Now let me express the material in my own words:

Badke argues that electronic documents are radically different from other things called "document." Electronic documents can instantly be seen everywhere on the Internet, people can alter them so that we have no idea what the original was, they can be linked to other electronic documents, and the order in which you read them may not be important.

What I have done is to ***interpret*** what I've read and express it mostly in different words (though it's all right to use a few words from your source, maybe 5% or less).

> **Remember, though, that the main point of a research essay is not simply to quote or interpret others, but to evaluate their work and provide your own arguments. Your analysis is extremely important.**
>
> **The professor in a Western academic setting is mainly interested in seeing how well YOU have understood the material. Professors do not want you simply to repeat what you've read but to interpret what you've read, expressing your own understanding in your own words.**

But what if your English is not very good, and other writers have already expressed their thoughts in better grammar than you could ever use? The answer is that you still need to use your own words except for brief quotations.

# A Short Note on Copyright

Copyright is a law that is intended to prevent people from making copies of published books and articles (or parts of these) without permission. Normally copyright law does not prevent a student from making quotations from published materials in a research essay as long as the student essay does not quote more than about 10% of a published work.

Students do, however, break the copyright law when they copy a major part or all of a published book or when they copy several articles from the same issue of a journal. Your school will likely have a statement about copyright available to guide you.

# 8

## *Other Types of Assignments—Reading Assignments, Book Reviews, Journals, Reflection Papers, Group Projects, Seminar Presentations, Class Participation*

When you first look at your syllabus, you will probably be concerned about the number and variety of assignments that are listed. Research papers are one type, but how do you do a reflection paper? This chapter will offer some guidance on how to complete assignments that may seem strange to you.

When you encounter an unusual assignment, the first thing you should do is check to see whether or not your professor has provided instructions along with the assignment. If not, it is certainly all right to ask him/her what is expected. When you do have instructions, either written or oral, follow them. Only use the suggestions below if you have no instructions from your professor or the instructions you received are not detailed enough to help you.

# Reading Assignments

Many courses offer grades for completing reading. Increasingly, however, professors will not simply accept a statement from you, "Yes, I did all the reading." In many cases, reading assignments are scheduled to be completed before particular classes so that the professor during class can question students on their understanding of or response to what they read. This means that reading must be done and done well, or you risk losing marks. In other cases, reading reports are required or the content of your reading will be included in the final exam. At times, you will be asked to write a book review (see below).

For international students, reading is a challenge. It takes more time than you have available, and it's very tempting to avoid reading everything. But the reading is a very important part of your education, and you need to take it seriously unless there is no time in your schedule to complete it, and the grade awarded for reading is very low (see Chapter Four, under "The Syllabus.") Perhaps a course in rapid reading would help you, but you should not do less than your best to complete it well.

# Book Reviews

Book reviews are intended to give you opportunity to evaluate something you are reading. There are standard methods of doing reviews. Knowing these can make the difference between success and failure.

But first, make sure you understand the difference between a *book review* and a *book report.* A book report is generally simply a summary of the book you read. It's intended to show that you read and understood the book. A book review includes a summary but goes on to evaluate the book, its good points and its bad, as well as its overall value. But here's a problem—some professors may use the term "book report," when they actually mean "book review." If you have any questions which type of assignment the professor is assigning, ask if this assignment to be just a summary or an evaluation.

A book review majors on evaluation and thus requires skills of critical thinking. You can't simply say that you liked or did not like the book. You must give reasons for your evaluation, provide evidence that your view is justified.

So just what is in a book review?

- **Bibliographical Information**—you need to provide a full bibliography statement for the book at the top of the review, using whatever bibliography style your professor prefers. It might look like this:

  William B. Badke. *Research Strategies: Finding Your Way Through the Information Fog.* Lincoln: Writers Club Press, 2000.

- **A summary**—Though a book review is not a book report, it must devote at least one-third of its space to explaining (without any evaluation) what the book is about. Evaluation comes later. What you want to do is give your reader a good understanding of the author's purpose in writing the book, the major subjects covered, and the author's conclusions. Remember, do not evaluate in the summary. Try to explain the book without revealing what you liked or did not like about it.

- **Positive Evaluation**—Now explain the features of the book that you believe are good or helpful. Did the author present a new approach to the topic that was believable? Did the author explain the subject clearly? Were there parts of the book that you appreciated, such as a good introduction, strong use of notes and bibliography, a good conclusion, or a helpful index? These are the sorts of questions you should ask.

  How much of the review will deal with positive evaluation? That will depend on what you discover. If you find that the book is excellent in many ways, you will devote most of the rest of the review to positive evaluation. If there is little good to say about the book, and many negative criticisms, your positive evaluation will be short. But do try to provide at least a paragraph of the positive before moving on to the negative.

- **Negative Evaluation**—now you need to point out problems or weaknesses in the book. This is often difficult for international students. If the book was assigned as a reading, the professor must have believed it was valuable to read. Why would you say anything negative about it? But the fact is that no book is perfect. If you are to show that you are a discerning reader who does not simply accept everything you read as wonderful, you are going to have to learn the skills of finding the problems.

  Negative evaluation is challenging. You must not only state what you disagree with. You must provide evidence to show that your negative view is correct. That evidence needs to go beyond feelings and into the world of facts and information. You need to be convincing enough to have your reader believe that there is good reason for evaluating the book the way you did.

  What should you be looking for? The first thing required is that you really understand what the author is intending to accomplish in the book. You cannot blame the author for not covering what s/he never intended to cover or for taking the subject in a direction that you do not like. The author determines the purpose or goals of the book. The sorts of questions you need to ask are:

  - Does the author actually accomplish what s/he promised? If not, what is missing or what has gone away from the stated purpose?

  - Are there statements that you believe are just incorrect? What evidence do you have that they *are* incorrect?

  - Does the author ignore information that might contradict his/her beliefs?

- Does the author explain anything poorly? Does s/he use language that is too complicated or ambiguous (could be understood in more than one way), or does s/he leave too much up to the reader by not explaining enough?

- Are there additional features—a bibliography, indexes, illustrations, etc.—that are not there, though you would normally expect in a book like this to have them?

- **Final evaluation**—In a final paragraph or two make a statement about the overall value of this book. Is it the best book ever written on the subject? Is it still a useful book despite some failings? Is it of such little value that you would not recommend it to anyone? Be careful about choosing an extreme, such as the first and last question above, too early. Most published works do have value despite a few flaws. It is a rare book that is simply excellent or simply terrible.

# Personal Journals

A journal is a diary, a day by day record of events. You might be keeping a diary yourself right now, recording the things that have happened during your day or your own reflections on daily life. An academic journal, however, is different from a personal diary. Let me give you some examples:

- Your professor tells you to do a journal along with your research paper, indicating the steps you took to decide what you wanted to write about, how you did the research, how you developed your outline, and so on. You can likely complete this by recording each step you take as you complete your project. But a journal needs as well to include your personal reflections on your experience as you go along—the struggles you have, the feelings these create, and so on.

- Some courses have a field component in which you participate in a company or organization outside of the classroom for anything from a few hours to a week or more. You may need to prepare a journal to record your experiences, including both events and your own reflections.

A journal could be part of any project or experience in the course. Its purpose is to get you to record your personal development or growth in the subject of the course. It assumes that you are not just learning facts but are actually being changed as you experience the various parts of the course. Your own reflections on your responses to what you have experience are very important. Once again, you can see that Western education values your own views and analysis highly.

## Reflection Papers

Reflection papers are a combination of the work done in a book review and the personal features of the journal. A reflection paper asks you to respond to something you have been asked to read or to some other learning experience (like a video or a guest lecturer). While you can explain the content of what you read, saw or heard, the main task is to reflect on it, to offer a personal response. Perhaps you disagreed with something and wanted to suggest an alternative. Maybe you agreed with everything and it caused you to think of something further that you want to say about the topic. As with both the book review and the journal, this assignment calls on you to go beyond repeating content into the world of personal thinking. What the professor wants to see is your *reaction*.

## Group Projects

Group projects can be worrying for international students. In a group project, you are not just responsible to produce your own assignment but to contribute, within a group of students, to the production of a project for which each person in the group will receive the same grade. If the others in your group are all Western, you may wonder if you can work with them well or make a real contribution. What if the others see you as someone without much to offer? What if they believe they did all the work and you contributed very little?

But before you become discouraged, think about some of the special things you can offer a group. You come from another country. You have a different view of many things in life. You have had experiences that others in the group have not. All of this can make you a valuable member of the team.

The first thing you need to do, before you even meet with the group itself, is to go over the requirements of the assignment very carefully. What is the topic? How are you supposed to do the research? Is there any indication of how each member is to contribute? What is the product going to be?

Your group, even if it is very small, will likely choose a leader. Do not expect that the leader will offer you a lot of guidance on how to do your part. The leader will not do most of the work either but will try to make sure the project is moving ahead and all members are making a contribution.

If you are asked to be a leader, you will need to work with the members of your group to determine which member is doing which part of the task. It will be your job to set a schedule to make sure the project is completed on time and to check to be sure that group members are on schedule. At the same time you will be doing your own part of the project. You will also need to direct the way in which the various parts are brought together into a final report, though you may find that someone else in the group wants to write the final report.

All of this means that you have a decision to make about how much you want to contribute to the project. In many groups there is at least one member who contributes very little and lets the other group members do most of the work. You could be that member, telling yourself that you are an international student, your English is not good, and you don't really know much about doing group projects. Or you could get totally involved, making an equal contribution by using the advantages that your background and culture bring to the project. If you made the last choice, you would actually be able to benefit from the learning experience.

The last choice is by far the best. As you get involved, you will find that the assignment helps you develop your skills at working in a team, as well as contributing work to a larger project. Don't let your fear of not knowing what to do prevent you from taking an opportunity to grow in knowledge and skill.

How do you carry out a group project?

- Look at what needs to be done and think about what part of the project would be easiest for you to do. As the group members are choosing their tasks, don't wait for others to choose first, or you will end up with only one choice, which will be the most difficult part. Instead, choose right away. This isn't selfishness. You are facing challenges in your education that students born in the West are not. Thus you need to make sure you choose first the task that will give you a good chance to make the best contribution you can.

- Consult with other group members about what your task involves. Don't just go and do it because you're worried that other group members will criticize you if you don't understand the task immediately. Say something like this to the group, "Before I get started, I want to be sure I know what I'm supposed to do. Could some of you tell me what you think my task is, so I can be sure I understand it?" In this way, even if you have misinterpreted your task, you won't have to let the other group members know what your misinterpretation was. Instead, get them to tell you what they think the task is. Then you can compare their understanding with yours.

- Find out what the schedule is and stay on schedule. If you discover you are falling behind, let the group leader know so that you can work out a solution together.

- As you complete various parts of the project, show these to the group leader so that, if there are any problems, you can correct them. There is nothing worse than bringing all your work to the group at the end only to discover that there are serious flaws in it.

- Remember that this is a group project. Stay in contact with the group constantly and consult with other group members on a regular basis. Learn to cooperate with others in the group and work for a common goal.

## Seminar Presentations

A number of polls have been taken to determine what are the greatest fears that people have. Number one consistently is the fear of public speaking. Very few of us feel at all comfortable getting up in front of others and making a speech. Yet most jobs involve some public speaking, even if it is simply presenting ideas to a few others with whom you work.

A seminar presentation is your opportunity to work at overcoming the fear of public speaking. Generally, a seminar presentation requires that you do a research project, present your findings to your professor and fellow students in class in anywhere from ten minutes to half an hour and then respond to questions from the students or the professor. It is thus a combination of a research paper, a speech and an interview.

For some international students this is the most challenging of all assignments. Not only will your research project be judged in public, but you will have to speak to your classmates and (an even more frightening thought) to your professor. This seems utterly backward. Should not the professor be doing the teaching? That's what you pay your fees for, so that the professor will teach you. And now s/he is asking *you* to be the teacher? This is certainly not fair or right. How can a mere student have anything to teach others? How can you call this education?

Yet it is certainly education, for the following reasons:

- You get the opportunity to improve your research skills and knowledge by preparing the content of the seminar.

- You learn how to organize material for public presentation.

- You get practice in public speaking.

- You receive the evaluation of your professor. While you might be assuming that a seminar is just a way for your professor to take a vacation, s/he is actually evaluating everything you do. If you are blessed with a good professor, you will get lots of feedback that will help you know both how you did and how you can improve for the next time you do an assignment like this.

Rather than dreading a seminar presentation, you need to think of it as an opportunity for growth. If you prepare well, everything should go well, though with public presentations there are never any guarantees. Remember that your fellow students are as uncertain about this experience as you are.

So how do you prepare well?

- Though this may sound very obvious, read the assignment very carefully. Be absolutely sure you understand it. In fact, even if you think you do understand it, find another class member who you trust and go over the assignment with him/her to see if you both understand it in the same way. If there is any doubt, check with the professor.

- Break the assignment into parts by determining what you have to do first, next, etc., then write down a schedule to help you be ready on time for your presentation. For example, if you need to do some background reading first, determine how long that will take and write that down. Then decide how much time the preparation of the material will take. If you are planning to use overheads or PowerPoint or some other visual aid, schedule time to prepare those things. You may not need to use visual materials, but they can help your presentation. Overhead transparencies are easy to prepare, and a computer presentation is not that difficult. Be ready with all written and presentation materials at least one week before your presentation day.

- Rehearse your presentation. Don't just write some notes for yourself and go over the presentation in your head. Find a quiet room where you can make the presentation aloud completely. If your professor has told you the presentation must be done within a certain time period, then time your presentation so that it will take exactly as long as the professor wants it to take. Rehearse it again and again, but don't memorize it—memorization will make your presentation sound too mechanical, not real. Rehearse your presentation until you feel comfortable with it, then rehearse it a few more times.

- If there is going to be a question and answer period after your presentation, it is possible that you could be asked a wide variety of questions. To prepare for this go over all of the notes from your research. Then try to think of possible questions that others in your class or your professor might ask. Rehearse possible answers. But be aware that there will likely be some questions you are not expecting.

The presentation itself will likely create anxiety for you, but there are things you can do to make it go well:

- Take care to eat and sleep well for several days before the presentation.

- Be sure that, if you have any visual presentations, the proper equipment is in the room and will be available to you. Find out how soon before the presentation you can get into the room to set up.

- Sit near the front of the room. When your professor introduces you and calls on you to present, you won't have far to walk before you are in place to present.

- If you are nervous, it's all right to tell that to the class. Remember that your fellow students will also be presenting either before or after you, so they will be sympathetic to your feelings. Try to set a light tone. What do I mean by this? Avoid being too formal and stiff. Make your presentation more like a conversation with the class. This will help you be less nervous.

- Be prepared for the possibility that not everything will go as you have planned. If you forget something, or your visual aids don't work, don't panic. Simply adapt to the new situation and go on with the presentation.

- Keep your eye on the time and do not go longer than you are allowed. If you find that you have spent too much time on the early part of the presentation, leave some things out of the later part and finish on time.

- If you feel comfortable with this, come from behind the podium or desk and stand in front of it when the question and answer time comes. Why? Because this part of the seminar is less formal, and moving away from the formal presentation place will help you feel more comfortable with answering questions for which you may not have prepared.

Seminar presentations may not be easy, but they really will help you grow. Consider them to be an opportunity rather than a problem. They will get easier the more of them you do.

## Class Participation

Group projects are done outside of class, and seminars are a special type of class participation, but some professors also assign a part of your grade to how well you participate in the class as a whole. This grade (usually 5–20%) is based on whether or not you were prepared (by doing reading assignments or other preparation), how well you answered questions, discussed issues in class, and so on. This is part of the emphasis on the classroom as a place of analysis and critical thinking in which views are raised, challenged and evaluated by students and professors alike.

Many international students find class participation grades unfair, because Western students have much less of a problem answering the professor's questions and entering into class discussions. But look at this as an opportunity to practice your speaking skills. Get away from the tendency simply to listen and learn without saying anything. You may find that the experience of participating may not be nearly as difficult as you first thought.

# 9

# *Quizzes and Examinations*

You have likely taken many examinations in your life, so you may be tempted to skip this chapter. But read on, because there are a number of suggestions that will help you improve your examination experience. Let's first consider the types of quizzes (short tests) and examinations (longer tests) that you may encounter. Then we will look at preparation methods.

## Pop Quizzes

Some professors like to make sure that their students are studying course material as they go through the course rather than leaving all study (called "revision" in some countries) until just before the final examination. Thus the "pop quiz" has been created. You and your fellow students will likely think of it as a cruel examination method, but it does have its value. Here is how it works:

The professor walks into class and announces, "Put all your books and papers under your desks. We're having a pop quiz." S/he will distribute sheets of paper with the questions on them, and you will write the answers. The factor that makes it a "pop" quiz is that it "pops" up without warning. You simply cannot predict when you will receive one, so you must keep up with your work at all times.

How do you make sure you do well in pop quizzes? First, near the beginning of the course, ask your professor (or listen to the answer when someone else asks), "Do you give pop quizzes?" Many professors do not, and the answer should tell you what to expect. In general, pop quizzes are more common in undergraduate classes than graduate.

Second, if your professor does give pop quizzes, stay up to date. This does not mean that you have to memorize your class notes every day, but at least read over them every evening. And be sure you don't skip classes when you know your professor does give pop quizzes. If you are not there when a quiz is given, your grade will be zero.

Pop quizzes may be troublesome, but they do keep students from being lazy. Don't resent them. Be ready for them.

## Scheduled Quizzes and Midterm Examinations

Other types of testing done during the semester are scheduled in your syllabus. You know when you are going to have to face that piece of paper with the questions on it. As an international student, however, you will likely have a special advantage—you've trained your memory in ways that most Western students have not. Thus, remembering your class material is easier for you than many other students who have trained their skills in critical thinking and analysis, not memory.

But there is a risk here. Unlike examinations in your homeland that stress remembering facts, examinations in the West, while using memory, will also ask you questions that test your critical thinking ability. What do I mean? Imagine that you are taking a course in modern European history. You have memorized all the significant dates and you know the common reasons for the beginning of World War I. But you may well be asked something like this: "Given the reasons for WWI, what could have been done to avert this war?" This is a question that you have not previously encountered, and you will have to think deeply to come up with an answer.

Such questions come from our Western emphasis on critical thinking. It is not enough that an examination tests what you know (facts). Examinations often also test how well you can think critically about what you know. This means that you may have questions that you have not considered in the classroom or your reading. Or you may have questions that have been discussed in class, but it is up to you to remember what the arguments were and how they fit together.

What, then, should you expect in a typical midterm examination?

- Short answer questions—matching questions, multiple choice, definitions, etc.

- Short paragraph questions—these usually test your understanding of a topic, but they may include some critical thinking.

- One or two longer questions—these almost always include both facts and critical thinking.

But you must recognize that no midterm examination is typical. Some professors prefer using all multiple choice questions, especially in undergraduate classes. Graduate examinations generally look for longer answers.

## Take Home Examinations

The take home examination is becoming rare, but you may encounter one. In this type of exam the student is given a set of questions and a time limit, generally two or three days. Students may use any source of information available, including the library, in order to answer the questions, but they may not consult with one another or any other person.

Typically, the questions in a take home exam are challenging and require critical thinking. They do not ask you to report the information you have covered in class but to go beyond that information, using what you have studied as a basis to discover new information and answer new questions. Do not assume that, because you have all sorts of research resources available to you, that you do not have to prepare for a take home exam. These exams are difficult, and the time to complete them is limited. Study at least the material you have received in class or readings. Then imagine possible questions that could be based on them and think about how you would answer them if you needed to on the take home exam.

## Final Examinations

A lot of students think final examinations are much more of a problem than midterm exams. While a midterm exam is generally only an hour long, finals are usually two hours and sometimes three. But the fact is that the two kinds of examination are very similar, with many of the same types of questions. The only differences are that you have a longer time to write a final and the mark usually counts more toward your final grade. What this means is that you need to take a final examination more seriously, but you will prepare for it the way you prepare for any other examination.

## Preparing for Examinations

In a moment I will provide you with suggestions for the best way to prepare for any examination. But first I want to explain the bad habit many students fall into.

The typical student does not begin thinking about exam preparation until a week or less before the date of the exam. S/he gets out class notes and other readings on which the exam will be based and "crams," that is, tries to memorize or at least become familiar with as much information as possible. Little thought is given to critical thinking questions. The student simply tries to absorb as much information in the short time left before the exam as s/he can. This likely involves late nights and a lot of coffee.

The result of cramming is that the student keeps the information temporarily in his/her memory, but that information is usually gone in a few days. What is more, cramming creates great stress, especially if the student waits too long before beginning and finds that there is not enough time to absorb all the knowledge needed to write the exam. Cramming often results in real lack of preparation for the examination.

What is more, cramming focuses on memory rather than critical thinking. Thus the student is not prepared to answer questions that require analysis.

You may already know how to study well for a coming examination. The steps you probably follow are these:

- Every evening through the semester, go over all the class notes and reading you have done for the day, making sure you read it through at least twice.

- At least once a week, take an hour or two to review all class notes and reading you did for the past seven days.

- At least two weeks before the coming examination, begin making outlines and summaries of your class notes, focusing on making sure you can define all important words, explain important concepts, and memorize significant lists, such as reasons why an event occurred, or the main features of a particular theory. Take special note of anything you have trouble remembering.

- As you prepare your material, begin thinking of possible critical thinking exercises that may be involved. For example, if you are in a psychology class that is studying the views of various therapists, you might guess that there will be a question asking you to compare and contrast the view of Freud and Adler on the nature of the unconscious. A history class might ask you to assess the reasons why a certain event happened.

- Do not cram. Do everything in your power to reduce stress. This means avoiding study after 10:00 pm, getting lots of sleep and exercise, and eating properly. The healthier you are, and the more rested, the less you will be troubled by anxiety during the exam. You will be alert and able to think clearly. In fact, during the hour or two before the exam, go for a walk, and enjoy yourself. This will leave you feeling refreshed when you start to write.

In a Western school, it is very unlikely that you will be given sample examinations to study. Most professors have their students return all examination papers and only provide to their students a final grade. Thus there are no sample papers to be found. If someone offers to sell you an examination in advance, you can be sure that this is illegal and that owning such an exam could result in severe punishment.

Shortly before examination time, it is almost inevitable that someone in class will ask the professor what will be covered on the exam. Most professors will provide some limited information on the topics that will be covered and the types of questions that may be encountered. Make sure you write down what you hear, but you can be sure that the professor will not tell you much.

There is one exception to this. Some professors will give the class, in advance, up to 10 questions that usually require both knowledge and critical thinking. The class is told that 3 or 4 of these questions will form the examination. In order to prepare for such an exam, you will have to write answers to each of the questions on your own before the exam, then study your answers. You will not be able to bring your answers into the examination room. When you get to the examination and discover which of the questions are on it, you will need to rely on your memory and your critical thinking abilities to write answers without the use of notes.

## Writing the Examination

Make sure you bring everything you need into the examination room—pens and any additional materials you are allowed to use in the examination. Do not bring your study notes and books.

Arrive at least fifteen minutes early so that you are sure you'll be on time, but try to find a place away from your fellow students, even if it means waiting outside the examination room. You want to spend the final minutes in quiet thought.

Above all, do not listen to the discussions of your fellow students, which will be along the lines of, "Do you know the date Napoleon was exiled?" or "I heard that there's going to be a question on the relationship between the Russian revolution and the end of WWI." Such discussions are an invitation to disaster, because they always remind you of parts of the course that you have not studied properly or possible exam questions you've never really thought about. All this does is add to your worry. Ten minutes before an exam is far too late for preparation. Stay out of the discussion.

Just before the exam time arrives, find a place to sit near the front of the examination room so that you will be able to read or hear instructions clearly. Don't assume that, because you've heard such instructions many times, they will always be the same. Pay attention to them.

When you are told you can begin, take the first five minutes to read through the entire exam and calculate the time you will need to complete each part in relation to the percentage each part is worth. For example, if there is a short definition section worth 20%, and you can do it in ten minutes, it may be better to start with that section than to start with an essay question worth 25% that will take you half an hour. This is also a good time to set some time limits for each part of the exam so you can complete it on time.

You do not have to write the exam in order it is presented. First do the questions that take the shortest time but are worth the most marks. Concentrate on getting easier parts done first. If there is a question you can't answer, leave it and move on. Perhaps some other question will help you recall what you've forgotten. Keep moving through the exam, even if you are finding that there are parts that are difficult to answer. Every time you run into a problem and you are not really getting far in your answer, though time is passing, leave it and go on to another one.

Once you have gone through the exam, go back to the questions you left earlier, first answering the ones worth the most. Don't panic. Now is the time to slow down and think deeply about your answers, because you are now working on the most difficult parts of the exam. Some students lose heart at this point and simply turn the paper in. Don't do that. Keep trying every question. If you are not sure of an answer, write down what you think the answer might be. If you get it wrong, you have lost nothing. If you have even part of it right, you can gain a few marks.

For longer answers, prepare a basic outline for yourself before you begin. This will keep you on the topic as you answer, and you can refer to the outline as you write so that you won't leave out anything that's important.

You may have some time left over. Use it to do two things. First, make sure all your answers are labeled properly on your answer paper—for example, section A., question 9. Second, read over your answers, making any revisions you think will be useful. But beware of a common problem called "second guessing yourself." In most cases, the first answer you wrote down is the correct one. But students often begin to have doubts when they read the answer again, and they change it. Unless you have very good reason for believing your first answer was wrong, leave it unchanged. But do revise your wording on longer answers to make them clearer.

Examinations are rarely enjoyable experiences. But if you prepare well, keep well rested, and don't panic while you're writing, you will likely get good results. Hopefully your good marks will be your reward.

# 10

## *Important People to Know in your Academic World*

Beyond your professors, you need to get to know a number of people on your campus. Why? Because each of them has services and resources to offer you that can help you succeed. Strangely, many international students avoid spending time with these people, preferring to stay within a small circle of friends. This is not wise. Those you meet and get to know in your educational experience are treasures in your treasure box. If you welcome them, your education will be rich. If you avoid them, your treasure will be small.

Who are these people? Let's learn about them.

## Your Faculty Advisor

When you registered, it is likely you were assigned a faculty advisor, often a professor. Your faculty advisor is there to help you make sure you are taking the right courses for your program and to offer guidance so that you can succeed in your studies.

Different institutions have different requirements for interaction with an advisor. Some insist that you meet with him/her at least once a semester. Others make your use of an advisor optional so that you only need to meet if you want to. Whatever the regulations, make sure you visit your academic advisor as often as you need to.

What can your advisor offer you? That varies, depending on the school you are attending, but it can include the following:

- Guidance to make sure you are taking the right courses, in the right order. True, you could get much of this information right from your school's website, but my experience is that very few students take a program of study in exactly the same way it is laid out in the website. It may be that a course you need is full, and you can't get in. This course may be required before you take another course in the same subject. Now what do you do? Your faculty advisor can tell you. It is also very important that you have someone like him/her available who can help you make sure you have actually taken all the courses required for your program.

- Guidance in choosing the number and type of courses you will take in any one semester. It may be that, while you are still gaining skill in the English language, you would be better to take three courses and do them well, instead of taking five and having great struggles. Your advisor can tell you the types of courses that are best to take—some have heavier workloads than others. Some courses are in a subject area with which you are familiar and some are not. It's always good to take a mix of courses so that only one or two of them are difficult in any one semester. You can discuss all this with your advisor.

- Help with developing your academic skills. Your faculty advisor can direct you to opportunities to improve your writing and speaking abilities, or offer you advice on how to improve your grades.

But be aware that your school's policy on the duties of faculty advisors may be different from what I've just outlined. Ask your advisor what services s/he is willing and able to give to you.

Note as well that most faculty advisors do this task in addition to courses they are teaching and research they are doing. Some consider it important work that they enjoy, while others see it just as a duty they must perform. Thus it is important to watch for signs that your advisor thinks s/he has given you as much time as s/he can (such as saying things like, "Well, thank you for coming," or "Is there anything else you needed?"—these are expressions calling for you to end the interview).

As well, always check your program requirements very carefully to make sure that you are actually taking all the courses you need. While it is uncommon, faculty advisors have been known to make mistakes. The responsibility for completing all your courses properly is yours.

## The Writing Center

Most Western schools have a writing center or an academic success center that is there to offer you guidance in improving your assignment skills. In some cases, you may meet with the same person each time you go there. In other cases, you will meet with different people. But you need to get to know these people.

Early in your first semester, go to the center and introduce yourself. Ask what services it offers. The people there will likely have a brochure or website that explains what they can do for you. This could include:

- Help with understanding and beginning your writing assignment. Bring a copy of your assignment and ask for assistance in developing the main theme and outline. In some cases, you can submit your question by e-mail and get an e-mailed response.

- Help with developing your assignment. You may already have some good ideas about what you want to know, but you're not be sure just how to turn these ideas into a paper. Bring a copy of your assignment along with everything you've written about the assignment so far. Write down your ideas and bring them with you to the writing center.

- Help with revising a draft of the whole paper, including structure, grammar, bibliographic format, and so one. *But take note*: Most writing centers will not go beyond pointing out problems or offering you some information about correcting your format. They will not make the corrections for you. They want you to learn how to improve your work by doing the revisions yourself.

- Short courses on research papers writing, proper bibliographical format, class presentations, and so on. Not all schools offer these, but many do.

  Remember, though, that writing centers are not places where you can get your writing done for you. The people at the writing center want to give you guidance, but they expect you to do your own writing and your own correcting. They want you to work hard at improving your skills. Most centers have limits on how many times you can visit and how long, so that you will not begin to depend on them too much. But you should to use whatever help they have available for you.

  Recently there have been controversies about international students using outside agencies or consultants to help them with their research papers. These agencies, for a fee, will often offer much more service than a writing center would, but they also do too much of the work that *you* are supposed to be doing. Students have successfully been penalized for plagiarism because they used a consultant who did most of the production of their research paper. Avoid these people. They are there to make money from you, not to help you learn how to write. Use the writing center instead, even if the center makes you prepare more of the assignment yourself.

# Student Services/Student Affairs

The student services or student affairs department of your school deals with all sorts of needs that are not academic. Why, then, would it help your academic success if you got to know the people at student services? Simply because you are not just a human brain. You are a *person* with many human needs. Student services, by helping you with other issues in your life besides academics, can give you the means to continue doing your academic work well.

When you first arrive on campus, Student Services staff will often organize tours of campus and explain to you the opportunities they offer, such as:

- Medical help—Even if there is not a doctor on campus (and there often is), there will likely be nurses who can offer you advice on any medical problem you may be facing. If you are not feeling well or if you have been injured, it is not wise simply to wait until you are better. Even a few days of not being able to go to class or do assignments could create great difficulties for you. Get medical help as soon as you need it.

- Counseling—In many countries, perhaps even your home country, people who need to see a psychologist are considered mentally ill and are thus seen as weak or unstable. In the West, psychologists are available to help anyone work through a problem and deal with life more successfully. The great majority of clients who see a psychologist have no mental illness at all. Why would you want to see a psychologist? Perhaps you are missing your home very much and your feelings of sadness are keeping you from getting your assignments done. Perhaps you have had some bad experience in your studies, and you are losing hope that you will ever succeed as a student. Perhaps you are starting to have panic attacks (sudden feelings of great fear) that are getting in the way of going to classes. Perhaps you have had a conflict with another person, and you are having difficulty understanding how to heal the division that has been created. Perhaps you simply want someone to explain Western ways that are confusing you and preventing you from doing well in your new culture.

In the West, going to a counselor is not a disgrace. Many students visit counselors for a variety of reasons. If you allow the problems that you are having to go on, you may find that you can't complete your courses. See a counselor, and don't be too proud to get the help you need.

- Student success—Short courses and seminars could be available to improve your abilities as a student (study skills, time management, speed reading and so on). Check with your student services office to see what is being offered.

- Social events—What do parties and banquets and concerts have to do with academics? A great deal. You simply cannot study all the time. Events that are fun and give you a chance to interact with other students can be very important to a balanced life that will allow your academic work to be stronger.

## International Student Services/Division

This department may go under several possible names but is intended to be there to provide for special student services help to international students. Services that may be offered include:

- Tours and seminars to orient you to western life.

- Guidance on western customs.

- English training opportunities.

- Specialized advice for problems related to being in a new culture.

- Partnership programs that help you meet with a Western student for English conversation and an opportunity to learn about one another's cultures.

  The people in this department understand the challenges you face and are available for advice or simply to listen to you. Get to know them well. The better you are able to deal with being a stranger in a new culture, the better you will be able to keep your academic success going.

## Reference Librarians

I am a reference librarian who meets often with international students at the information desk. Many international students spend a great deal of time struggling with how to use the library or how to do research, but they are afraid to ask the reference librarian on duty for help. This isn't much different from Western students—asking for help is hard for anyone. But you have a great deal more to lose if you avoid the reference librarian, because you are still learning to use library systems that many Western students are already familiar with.

I find that students (Western or international) who come to the reference or information desk for help often begin with a question that is not the real question they want to ask. For example, they may ask, "How can I find journal articles?" when what they really need is five articles on the Taliban of Afghanistan. I think students are afraid to ask specific questions because they worry that the answer will take too much of the librarian's time. So they ask a general question that is easily answered and hope that once they know how to find journal articles, they will be able to find articles on the Taliban by themselves.

We reference librarians know very well that the first question you ask is not likely to be the question you really need answered. So we ask questions in return: *What subject area are you looking for? Do you have an assignment that requires you to have journal articles? Do you have a copy of the assignment or can you explain it to me?* We are not trying to make your life difficult. Instead, we are trying to discover what you really need to know so that we can make your life easier.

It's better, then, to come to the reference librarian with a specific question. Here are some suggestions:

- If your question relates to an assignment, bring your syllabus with you and show the assignment to the reference librarian.

Explain what part of the assignment you are having difficulty with in the library.

- International students are often dealing with unfamiliar words or strange names that are found in an assignment. When they come to the reference desk, they have difficulty pronouncing those words or they are not sure just how to phrase their question. I have had the experience many times of simply not being able to understand what the student is asking. I don't recognize the pronunciation or the question does not make sense to me. If you come to the reference desk without your assignment, take a few moments to *write* down the question you want to ask. This will greatly help the reference librarian to understand what you need.

- If you have a question about an assignment or you need to know how to use a database, make sure you actually receive a useful answer from the librarian before you proceed on your own. Some reference librarians, especially if they are busy, may cut their answers short. Have courage and ask more questions until you really know you have an answer. If you find later on that you need further explanation, do not hesitate to return to the reference desk.

- Reference librarians usually have specific hours of duty. If you find a librarian that is especially helpful, take note of when that person is on duty so that you can return to him/her when you have another question. But be careful that you don't just use the librarian's time in friendly conversation not related to problems in your research. Librarians have a job to do that is very specific, and they are often short of time for conversation not related to your research. But they are happy to help you with any project you are working on. That's their job.

A reference librarian can be one of the most important people you know on campus. Be brave and ask your questions. You will find that most librarians are very helpful. They are well trained, usually with one or more masters degrees, and their knowledge of the library and computer systems is excellent. They can help you find the right subject heading to use in the catalog, guide you in starting a research project, explain how to use a periodical index, or tell you more about library operations. As such, they are valuable people indeed.

## Your Fellow Students

I want to raise a difficult cultural issue. Students who grew up in a certain place tend to feel most comfortable with people from their homeland. International students, like any students, tend to be happiest finding friends from their own culture. Thus in a Western university cafeteria you will often find groups of Chinese students, Korean students, Nigerian students, and so on, spending time together. But, while you enjoy being with friends who are like you, the best way to develop English speaking ability, understanding of Western culture and the skills of being a student in the West, is to develop friendships with Western students.

Introduce yourself to others in your classes who are not from your culture. Have lunch with them. Study with them. The more you step outside of your own group and open yourself to relationships with Western students, the more you will find that your basic skills for being a successful student in the West will grow.

Here is some advice offered by a number of international students at the University of British Columbia (**http://students.ubc. ca/international/handbook/succeed/**):

- Take the opportunity to see instructors.

- Ask more questions.

- Be proactive—ask for help.

- Be curious and seek information.

- Connect with senior students.

- Speak with advisors and professors.

- Take advantage of the services available.

- Get involved.

- Be assertive when you need something.

- Don't isolate yourself; get involved in a "small community"—clubs, groups.

# CONCLUSION
## Encouragement

- You are *intelligent*. If you were not, you wouldn't have been accepted into the school you are attending.

- You have *motivation*. There are not many people brave enough to leave their culture and study in another one, using a language that is unfamiliar and difficult.

- You have the *endurance* to continue struggling in a challenging setting until you have completed your education.

I admire you for following your dream and overcoming obstacles to do so. Yet there are likely going to be many times when you wonder if you made the right decision by traveling all these thousands of miles to study.

I recently received e-mail from an international student who was discouraged because my comments on his research paper had said so little about what was good and so much about what was wrong in his lesson. That was a lesson to me to include more encouragement in my comments, but the fact is that you may receive back research papers with negative comments, and you are going to have to learn how to deal with discouragement. You will have to risk embarrassment in the classroom, possibly racism among others on campus, and grades that are lower than you feel you deserved.

In the midst of all this, remember the reasons why you came to the West to study. Remember your dreams and those of your family and friends at home. Remember the sacrifice that you and others have made to get you here. You have committed too much effort to give up easily now.

It is very tempting, when things get difficult, to look for the wrong solutions, like plagiarism or other forms of cheating. Do not give in to such temptation. It would be terrible to be sent home because you were expelled for cheating. It would be even more terrible to know that others actually earned your degree for you.

While you can't get others to do your work, don't avoid seeking the proper help of others. You probably believe that it is your duty to independent and solve all your own problems. You may believe that looking for help from a professor or advisor or librarian or student services worker is a sign of weakness. It is not. Seeking help is simply using the opportunities that have been given to you to increase your chance of succeeding. If help is available, and using it is not cheating, use it. If you find yourself getting so discouraged that it is preventing you from getting your studies done, see a counselor. Your program of study is too important for pride to prevent you from getting help.

Make good friends with fellow students both from your homeland and from the West. Friends can encourage you when you've had a bad day, and their wisdom can help you find solutions to your problems. If you have a religious faith, find those who practice it and seek them out as a further community of support.

There is every reason to believe that you will succeed. You have passed the entrance requirements to your school and you have shown strong motivation to be here. There are three characteristics that a student needs to succeed—intelligence, motivation, and endurance. You have already shown that you have all three. Thus there is no reason to give up, no matter how difficult your studies become. There is every reason to believe that you can complete your program successfully.

Remember that everyone—your family and friends, your professors, and the administrators of your school—want you to succeed. They have provided you with support so that you can do so.

Be encouraged. You can have academic success just like the many other students who have gone before you. Just use the gifts you already possess, and never give up.

If you wish to contact me to tell me about your experiences as an international student, please e-mail at badke@twu.ca.

# Appendix

## *Graduate Study and Thesis Work*

The following is not a handbook to graduate studies. Nor is it a thesis manual. I simply want to make some observations about life as a graduate student in the West. Most of the skills needed to succeed have already been described in this book, but there are some elements of graduate work that are different.

## Expectations

The movement from undergraduate to graduate level studies often creates a dramatic change in what professors expect from students. Let's consider some of the elements of this change:

- Critical thinking. Undergraduates are encouraged to think analytically and to evaluate everything they hear and read. But graduate students are expected to do more of this on their own. In the classroom and in their writing, graduate students should be prepared to notice problems related to a certain point of view, then consider the various options and determine which is the most likely to be correct. If you struggle with thinking critically on your own, you would benefit greatly from a course or seminar on critical thinking.

- Amount of work. Graduate students find that the number and size of assignments are greater than they were in undergraduate days. Since you have no more hours in your week than you did when you were an undergraduate, you will have to become more efficient with your time. For some students, this seems to mean that they need to bring an end to their social life. Rather than take time to relax or be with friends and family, they work all the time on their course assignments. This is not a good idea. It simply actually creates more stress that makes it harder to complete the course work.

The alternative is to develop skills that help you to do the work more quickly while at the same time making sure it is of good quality. What skills will help you?

- Rapid reading or speed reading. Take a short course in either, and you will find that you can get your reading assignments and your reading for research done more quickly. Remember, though, that this is no substitute for working on your English at the same time. Speed reading does not help if you have to stop constantly to remember what certain words mean.

- Improvement of English language skills. Keep on developing your English language ability, not just your reading, but your speaking. For spoken English, one of the best things you can do (better than taking a course) is spend time in conversation with Western students.

- Time management. If you find that you have trouble organizing your time properly, do some reading on time management. You will find that there are many things you can do to make the better use of every moment of your day.

- Personal health. If you do not keep a proper diet, if you refuse to exercise because you don't have time, or if you don't get enough sleep, you will quickly find that even when you are working on your courses, you are not doing it well. In fact, it may take you longer to get an assignment done simply because your body is not well. Take care of your body so that you have the energy to get the most out of the time you have.

- Level of work. By level of work I mean the quality of the work you do. In graduate school, you are expected to deal with more difficult concepts, do deeper thinking, and write papers that are similar to those in scholarly journals, though not quite as sophisticated. Simple answers and research papers with only six items in the bibliography are not going to succeed. Graduate students must think for themselves.

This will likely make you feel some doubts about yourself. How can someone from another country, with language difficulties, possibly perform at a level almost as high as the professor's? The first thing you need to do is recognize that graduate study asks you to make a transition in which you need to take personal responsibility for your studies like you never have before. Many graduate students are surprised at how much scholarship is required. Don't be surprised. Expect it and make yourself ready.

How can you prepare? Start by reading a few journal articles in the subject area you will be taking for your program. Try to understand how scholars in that subject express themselves, how they think. Take a look at the kinds of resources they use in their bibliographies. At the masters level, you will likely be allowed to use research materials that are mainly in English, though reading knowledge of another European language may be required. For doctoral studies, you often need a reading knowledge of one or more other languages. Talk to graduate students who are working in your subject area, if you can find them, and learn from them about the skills you require. When you get into your program, look for other students who are not necessarily from your culture, but who will be willing to study with you so that you can learn and develop depth in your studies together.

- Amount and level of reading. You will to strengthen your English reading skills because you will be reading more, and what you are reading will have more difficult terminology.

- Complexity and length of research papers. Your papers will be longer and will call for more research. Now you will need to read primary sources (those directly written by the significant people of the past in your subject area) as well as secondary sources (those written later and commenting on the work done by people in the past). Your bibliographies will grow to 15, 20, 50 references or more, depending on how long your papers become. Periodical literature will always be expected.

## The Graduate Experience

Graduate students find themselves in a different world from that of undergraduates. In undergraduate days, your professors had to encourage you to complete your assignments on time and follow proper procedures. You were told how to do your work and how to prepare for your exams.

Graduate studies place more responsibility on *you* in the selection of your courses, the way you do your assignments, your attendance in classes, and the way you complete your program. You are expected to be a well-motivated student who can be trusted to do his/her studies with a minimum of prodding from the professor.

You, your professors, and your fellow students work together in a closer learning relationship than you have been used to. You are more likely to call the professor by his/her first name and to be treated by your professor as someone who has a significant contribution to make to the subject area you are studying. Your professor is more like a colleague than a lecturer. You will find that you, your fellow students and your professor will often enter into discussions in class that make you all seem like equals.

Your professor does have an important part in your education, however. S/he is a specialist in the subject you are studying, someone who has more experience and knowledge than you do. Thus your professor can correct your errors and guide you to deeper understanding. You need to think of professors at graduate level like older brothers and sisters who believe in your abilities and want to help you succeed. Listen to what they have to say. While you may find yourself sometimes disagreeing with them, most often they will be right in what they tell you.

Continue to develop relationships with library staff as well. They can be of great help to you in improving the level and quality of your research.

There is a temptation as a graduate student to spend all your time studying, neglecting your relationships with others, not eating properly and getting too little sleep. Do not allow your studies to isolate you from your friends or to destroy your health. This is a sure path to damaging your ability to study. A balanced life, with time for others, good food, and enough rest, gives you the strength you need to succeed at your studies.

## The Thesis/Dissertation

Sometimes the terms "thesis" and "dissertation" are used to mean the same thing, but more properly a thesis is written at the masters level and a dissertation at the doctoral level. Masters theses demand a great deal of original, critical thinking, and dissertations call for even more. Let's look at some factors of thesis writing, though you need to find one of the many books that can give you detailed guidance on thesis/dissertation preparation. Here are the basics:

- The Thesis Committee. This committee will oversee all parts of your work, from acceptance of your first proposal to final examination. The committee is usually chosen by others and your experience with it may be friendly and helpful or it may be stressful, depending on who its members are. The rule is that you must listen to what your thesis committee tells you, and, as much as possible, follow its directions.

- The Idea. Every thesis begins with an idea—a problem you want to solve, a question you want to answer, an experiment you want to try. Where do ideas come from? That is very hard to say. Often an idea will be something you discover as you are taking other courses. A professor may suggest something that s/he has always wanted to study. If you are having difficulty finding an idea to be the center of your thesis, talk to other students in your program or visit a favorite professor and ask for suggestions. When the right idea finally comes to you, you will know it. The right idea will be something that will motivate you greatly. Do not simply take someone's idea if does not excite you. Remember that you will have to live with your idea for one to three years, so you have to know it interests you enough to carry you through to the end of your project.

- The Proposal. The proposal explains in a few pages what your idea is and includes your research question or thesis statement, an outline with details about what each part will cover, and a basic bibliography. It will be presented to your thesis committee who might reject it and ask for a new proposal, or return it for revisions before accepting it, or accept it right away. Do not be surprised if you need to do some revisions. The most important thing is to follow exactly the directions you have been given for preparation of the proposal. Don't be disappointed if your first proposal is rejected or revisions are asked for. This happens quite often, and not just to international students. Thesis work demands that you persevere, so don't give up. Revise your proposal as you are asked to and send it back to the committee until it is accepted.

- The Advisor. Your advisor will be a professor (chosen sometimes by you, sometimes by your committee, depending on the policy of your school) who has an interest in your subject area. The advisor may be chosen before your proposal is completed, but will most often start working with you when you have presented your proposal. *Listen to your advisor*. If you have the attitude that you know what you are doing and you resent anyone telling you that it needs changes, you will never complete your thesis. Your advisor is there because you don't know everything. Every thesis student needs an objective critic and guide who can tell you what is right and wrong, good and bad about your work and can help you improve. It is not your advisor's job to make you fail or destroy your self-esteem. S/he is there to make sure that you complete your work *successfully*. While there are never any guarantees, doing what your advisor tells you gives you the best chance of succeeding.

How much time will you spend with your advisor? That varies greatly. Some advisors may be well known and greatly respected professors, but they can give you only two or three hours per semester. Others may be not as well known, but they are available to you whenever you need them. This is something you should ask your advisor when you first meet him/her: "How much time are you available to me? How often do you want to meet with me?"

- The Work. Thesis work is like nothing you have ever done before. With most research papers in the past, you gathered the materials, wrote the essay, and then you were done with it. Thesis work, because it is much longer and more complicated, goes on an on. Your thesis comes to live in your house, and then starts to live in your heart. You find yourself distracted into thinking about it while you're eating, while you're with your friends, while you're taking a walk or watching a movie. You wake up in the middle of the night with some new thought about how you can develop your argument. This is not some kind of mental illness. In fact, it's perfectly normal and even necessary if you are ever to do your thesis well. Your thesis has to haunt you like a ghost before it means enough so you can create something of depth and power.

But beware. You still must keep a balanced life. You can't work on the thesis all the time if you are to remain strong enough to do the work required. Take breaks, even if your thesis is never very far from your thoughts.

Thesis work requires three characteristics from you if you are to succeed: intelligence, strong motivation, and endurance. All three characteristics are essential.

- The Examination. When you finally submit your thesis or dissertation to your thesis committee, you may be tempted to think that your work is done. But there is more to do. The written product will be sent to examiners (usually three), one of whom will likely be your advisor and another a person from another institution. They will read and evaluate your thesis independently of one another, then they will meet together to agree on a grade. They have three options—to reject the thesis (which is rare and usually comes only if you refused to follow the instructions of your advisor), to accept the thesis but ask for revisions before final acceptance is complete, or simply to accept the thesis with no revisions. Most students receive the second choice. It is rare to be asked for no revisions at all.

  The next part of the examination is usually called "the oral." You will be called to meet with the examiners for about two hours to answer their questions. The oral is a way for the examiners to confirm that the thesis is your own work and that you really did have the knowledge to complete it. You will be asked what your research question or thesis was and how you dealt with it in your paper. Your examiners may take you to parts of your thesis to ask you to clarify what you wrote or to challenge your argument and ask you to defend it. They might ask you questions about your knowledge of information covered in your thesis. This may seem like a challenging process, but if you have prepared by going over your thesis and research materials, you can do well. Your advisor will likely to be happy to guide you in advance on the best way to prepare for the oral.

Can you write a thesis or dissertation that will pass? Only you can determine this for sure. But if you have a good idea, listen to those who are guiding you, and refuse to give up, you improve your chances greatly and will likely end up with a good thesis. The key is to keep on trying until you succeed. That, of course, is the secret to every kind of academic success.

# Index

**A**

Assignment scheduling 53
Attendance in class 144

**B**

Bibliography style, *see* Form in Research essays
Book reviews 105, 106
Book reports, *see* Book reviews

**C**

Classification systems—Libraries 79
Computer 28, 30, 40, 41, 42, 50, 52, 72, 76, 77, 78, 85, 115, 134
Copyright 103
Courage 17, 18, 21, 34, 37, 48, 133
Critical thinking 3, 10, 11, 12, 22, 23, 24, 25, 26, 33, 35, 36, 38, 59, 65, 107, 117, 119, 120, 121, 122, 123, 141, 145

**D**

Discipleship Model of education 9, 11, 68
Discussions 26, 35, 36, 45, 117, 123, 124, 144
Dissertations, *see* Theses

**E**

English, Spoken 18, 19, 20, 21, 22, 36, 42, 60, 142
Essays, *see* Research essays
Examinations 2, 3, 16, 41, 52, 118, 119, 120, 121, 123, 125

**F**

Faculty advisor 126, 127, 128
Form in Research essays 93

**G**

Graduate study 141, 143

Group projects 36, 105, 110, 111, 116

**I**

International student services 131
Internet, *see* Computer

**J**

Journals, Personal 109

**L**

Labs 39, 40
Librarians, Reference 132, 133
Library 2, 3, 16, 23, 28, 46, 55, 59, 71, 72, 73, 74, 75, 76, 77, 78, 79, 80, 81, 82, 84, 85, 86, 94, 99, 120, 132, 133, 134, 145

**M**

Mediated learning 40, 41
Mentoring 68, 70
Midterm examinations, *see* Examinations

**N**

Note taking 26, 28

**O**

Office hours 60, 61, 62
Online courses, *see* Mediated learning

**P**

Participation in class 116, 117
Plagiarism 46, 97, 98, 99, 100, 129, 138
Postmodernism 11, 12, 13, 24
Presentations 16, 31, 38, 39, 105, 113, 114, 115, 116, 129
Professors 3, 6, 11, 13, 25, 26, 29, 30, 32, 33, 38, 41, 48, 56, 58, 59, 60, 65, 66, 67, 68, 69, 70, 87, 88, 89, 93, 98, 99,

103, 106, 116, 117, 118, 120, 123, 126, 135, 138, 141, 144, 147

## Q

Question answering 33
Quizzes 41, 52, 118, 119

## R

Reading assignments 52, 105, 106, 116, 142
Reflection papers 105, 110
Research essays 87, 95, 100

## S

Seminars, *see* Presentations
Student services 21, 28, 64, 129, 130, 131, 138

Syllabus 32, 41, 45, 46, 47, 48, 51, 61, 62, 86, 105, 106, 119, 132

## T

Take home examinations 120
Term papers, *see* Research essays
Theses 93, 145
Time management, *see* Assignment scheduling

## V

Virtual campus, *see* Mediated learning

## W

Western Model of education 9, 10, 13, 70
Writing center 59, 61, 62, 65, 128, 129

0-595-27196-0

Printed in the United States
1501100005BA/7

9 780595 271962